Road to Porterville by Len Dickson

Rita's Road

Rita's Road
Judi Loren Grace

Jetstream Publishing
Chico, California

Published by Jetstream Publishing in association with Memoir Books
Chico, California

Publications by Jetstream Publishing:
The Third Floor, Judi Loren Grace
Dreamscape in A minor, Judi Loren Grace
Rita's Road, Judi Loren Grace

Contact Judi Loren Grace: kepi@sunset.net
 Follow Judi Loren Grace on Facebook
jetstreampublishing.com

© 2014 Jetstream Publishing and Judi Loren Grace, all rights reserved.

ISBN: 9781937748142
Library of Congress Control Number: 2014947770

Printed in the United States of America

Cover Design: Connie Ballou, Back Alley Graphics
Interior Design and Layout: Connie Ballou, Back Alley Graphics
Painting *Road to Porterville*: Len Dickson
Copy Editor: LaDawn Black Hall

Contents

Dedication	VII
Acknowledgements	IX
Author's Note	XI
Book One	1
Murray's Digs	3
The Roach Gang	15
Hag Hollow	33
The Wilder Side of Me	51
Smoke Rings	63
Canada or Bust	79
Rita	93
The Prankster	103
Ode to GaGa	109
Dandelions in Overdrive	113
Late Bloomer	127
Book Two	137
The Long Pause	139
Onion Breath	149
Midnight Caller	167
Kindling	177
Tennis Balls and Apples	187
Mozie	201
Money Matters	215
Flying Solo	223
New Crush	237
Tijuana Rose	245
From the Heart	257

Dedication

Dedication of *Rita's Road* is bestowed to Miss Judith Murray Schmeichel.

When our world turned upside down, you stood strong against the harsh winds of misfortune, which swept most of us off a cliff. Murray, you kept the flames of friendship aglow both before and after Rita's life threatening and mind altering presence. You've shown us the true meaning of friendship with your compassion and your unwavering patience. Somehow you managed to sprinkle this uncharted territory with a keen sense of humor. Your appreciation and respect for Rita is constant and apparent. You listened to her night after night, year after year, as she struggled to find her inner self after the results of an unfortunate one second click. A click that altered a life.

Acknowledgements

A very special thank you to Bill and Genia Simpson for mailing Rita's treasured photo albums, scrap book, and very personal papers.

Bill, thank you for the color enhanced photos. You supplied many family details, dates and random bits of information, which helped to form a cohesive picture for Rita's story.

Bundles of love to Rita's niece Lisa Simpson Perkins and nephew Loren Simpson.

Special thanks to Ruth Ann Vance, Rita's caregiver and friend. Ruth Ann was Rita's saving grace and together they shared many laughs, and never ending chores. Ruth Ann relayed that Rita frequently and with great excitement shared many stories about her friends back home. Rita began each memory with clarification, referring to her teenage stories as, "my other life."

Thank you to Sue Harnley and Linda Phelps; the counselors who carefully and artfully reinforced Rita's joy and passion for living.

Also, big hugs and a heartfelt thank you to The Roach Avenue gang, and many other friends. Thank you for joyfully reliving and telling stories of Rita's travels, her unexpected explosive outbursts, and her deliciously dry humor. Rita's ridiculously naughty vocabulary intertwined with pranks and insults still swirl in our heads.

Fond memories to Rita's mother, Marie Simpson, who stayed focused and unruffled. Marie never lost her wickedly dry sense of humor through the shuffle and chaos of her life.

Honorable mention to GaGa, Rita's colorful and playful grandmother, willing accomplice, and teacher to all.

Thank you to Len Dickson for the use of his painting, *Road to Porterville*. This stretch of Highway 65 is the main connection between our hometown to Bakersfield and onto Los Angeles; Rita drove this road many times.

Behind every successful woman is a best friend giving her crazy ideas.

Author's Note

I was immediately drawn to Rita, especially her quick wit. We have a similar background, which borders on dysfunctional, and everything clicks with us. Our friendship is easy, and throughout our life, we remain steadfast friends.

Our friends are crazy, wild and easily bored. We do whatever it takes for a good laugh. Rita is our leader in crime and she alone teaches most of the people in our small town how to inhale and blow smoke rings. She is full of bad ideas with no boundaries. She is impulsive and the epitome of a true prankster. Her side kick is her Austin-Healy.

Our friends slowly disperse in many directions after high school graduation. One by one they leave the security of their homes and our small town. It is during this time Rita and I become family. I spend many nights at her house, just four houses down the street, running there with my tooth brush in hand, right past Leo's house. Her mother finally gives me a house key.

In her mid twenties everything changes. Her inner circle of lifelong friends stands strong in support. We become a faint memory as she struggles to remember who she is, and who she used to be.

Writing her story pulls me back to our time of antics and stimulating ideas. Here, alone at my desk as I type her story, I have to smile, giggle and sometimes laugh out loud.

Step back to the innocence of the early 1960s. Tag along on wild rides, weekends at Rita's cabin, trips into the city of San Francisco, and learn from our leader, *Tijuana Rose*.

This is a true story of friendship, teenage pranks, love, patience and Rita's fight of a lifetime.

Judi Loren Grace

Book One

THE CARS WE DRIVE SAY A LOT ABOUT US.
Alexandra Paul

Murray's Digs

SHE TOSSES OUR BAGS into the small trunk of her white Austin-Healey and we jump in. The seats are worn black leather with white leather trim. She surprises me with a bag of caramels and two bananas, which she tosses between my *Jesus sandals*. I'm no food expert, but I know caramels and bananas won't do well on a hot floorboard on a hot day, so I put them behind us in a little shaded cubby. It's the beginning of summer; the morning's cool breeze teases us with a few hours of refreshing air as if the afternoon sun won't melt us away. That's why we drive as fast as we can, "To beat the heat, Officer." We are already prepared in case we get stopped. It's the summer of 1964, school is just behind me, but Rita and Murray graduated a year before. Our future is at the threshold, beginning to unfold like a magnificent flower. Our choices and lives are wide open and the days seem endless.

School has been out for two months, and my choice for a successful life is Beauty College, which doesn't start until October. I check out Santa Rosa Jr. College and Porterville Jr. College, but feel the need to express myself artistically, make people look their finest. Rita works for a loan company, where she and a girl named Joyce sit in a back room. There is a dead fly stuck on the wall directly in front of them. They name it Sidney and talk to it every day, circle it with a pencil and decorate the circle with gold stars and tiny ribbons. Rita puts things around it to celebrate holidays. This seems to help with the monotony of pushing papers and the buttons on adding machines. Rita is casually investigating Heald's Business College in Fresno. We're in our late teens, not concerned about our approaching twenties because, from our point of view, things can only get better. And through the windshield of her windy Austin-Healey, our actual point of view is nothing but wide open space.

Our girlfriend Murray, who had recently dropped out after one year at Fresno State, made the big move to the Bay Area to enroll in the John Robert Powers modeling school. We're headed her way, and I can hardly wait to see what she looks like now.

When Rita starts the engine, a low rumbling roar surrounds us, sends vibrations throughout our bodies. Her prized car, her baby, begins to take us on a journey we'll never forget. She whips a U-turn on the street next to the side of her house, and off we go. The stage is set for a glorious road trip.

Rita has a heart of gold, though she gets pretty frustrated at times. When this happens, all she has to do is snarl and cuss her way back to cheerfulness, her normal state of mind. She is beautiful in her own boyish way. She has short curly hair the color of sand, high cheekbones and chiseled features. Her thin lips often wear a smirk, but her eyes are her winning feature. They are huge, expressive and green, with black lashes. She uses her thick eyebrows to her advantage when looking smug or evil. But she isn't evil; she is warm and always there for her friends. She is one of the rare people who can make each person she's with feel they are her best and only friend. I cherish Rita.

She happily turns onto the freeway and roars through the many small towns that dot the central valley. She follows the signs north for Sacramento. We rumble along with both loud music and the wind encircling us. She breezes past Fresno, Madera and other small agricultural towns. In what seems like no time at all, she exits to the right, and we cross the freeway overpass under a huge sign that reads: San Francisco. The air seems to change as we get closer to our destination.

Murray is at work all day, but has assured us she'll be home well before we roll in. The time doesn't concern us because we are free spirits with no clocks, but memories of past trips tell us we'll be pulling up to her abode in three to four hours. Murray doesn't care about the time either. She just tells us to be careful and not get a ticket.

Our excitement is infectious. Leaving our small town to stay with Murray will be a blast, but for Rita it also represents freedom from the dead fly on her office wall. This is my graduation gift to myself—a kick-off for the rest of my life. Plus, I get to hang out with two of the coolest chicks on the planet.

Our jaunt takes us over the rolling mounds of hills that look as if they were placed specifically for our visual pleasure. The further we go into the cut in the earth that makes up this highway, the narrower our view becomes. The mounds that once looked like hills now look like shiny, magnificent half-boulders formed by bulldozers. This four-lane stretch of winding road begins to gain elevation. As we roar over the top of the Pacheco Pass we are at 1,368 feet, compared to our hometown's 438 feet. We leave behind the central valley, where by now the heat is surely climbing and all of our friends will fry in a matter of minutes. For us the air is cool and sweet.

I allow my head to fall back so I can look straight up at a ceiling of crystal blue skies and two small clouds. I unwrap two caramels without looking, and pop them into my watering mouth, then slowly turn my head toward Rita and watch her hair as it swirls in every direction. She looks content; one arm rests on the window ledge, her other hand on the wheel, a cigarette between two fingers. The most noticeable sounds are the purr of the engine and the wind whipping around our heads. The radio has begun to cut out so now we hear static mixed in with the music. I can't help myself; I have to snap a picture of her driving.

The powerful churning wind rustles and dances through our hair and ballooning blouses, and the Beatles sing "I Wanna Hold Your Hand." This is one of Rita's favorite songs, and we sing at the top of our lungs. Then another one comes on, "I Saw Her Standing There." It's Beatlemania weekend. In a short time the radio station goes dead. I look over toward Rita again. Her cigarette is still intact. She takes a drag and blows smoke straight upward as she turns up the volume and hunts for a better station. She looks at me and yells in a voice just louder than the engine and wind, "Do you think you can find another station or are you too busy chewing caramels and staring at the sky?" I've never felt so free and happy in my life.

While we're cruising along, a metal flake midnight blue Buick full of guys tries to pass us in the fast lane. They reach out their windows, wave, and yell for us to pull over. *Right*, I think to myself, *pull onto the soft shoulder—are you idiots?* Rita puts her cigarette between her lips, slowly raises her left arm, and flips them the bird. I grin back at them so as not to make enemies of strangers. Rita floors it, and off we go, as fast as her Austin-Healey can move, leaving these poor guys in our dust. We both let out whooping screams from the power surge.

Rita has a smirk on her face and takes another drag from her cig. I put my arms up as high as they'll reach and let the wind carry me away. Off we go over the Pacheco Pass, speeding closer to *The City*. In a second, I find a new station, and life is perfect. We listen to "Leavin' on a Jet Plane" by Peter, Paul and Mary. Rita sings, "Don't know when I'll be back again," and I sing, "Oh Babe, I hate to go." We see the sign for Gilroy and this is the key point in the trip for me. This town is the gateway to *The City*. It's kind of far from home and kind of close to Murray's.

The approach to the inner city of San Francisco is an instant game changer. There are cars everywhere, trucks, highway patrol, freeways coming in, dumping more traffic into these lanes as cars merge ever nearer. Still, people look at us and wave or smile and honk. We smile back. Well, I do. Rita stays focused. The traffic makes me nervous and I am relieved not to be the driver.

Rita seems to have an antenna inside her head as she takes us to an exit, makes several turns up and over steep streets and back down again. I mean straight down, as if her car is a roller coaster on the Santa Cruz Boardwalk. She laughs out loud at my screams, so I peel a browning banana and eat it for security. Finally, she goes around a few corners, grabs the address that is crunched in the palm of my hand on a tiny shard of paper, pulls over to read it, then makes a few more turns.

Here we are at Murray's place near the corner of Jackson and Fillmore, just down the street from the bad part of town, but still in a very hip neighborhood. We get out, stretch, and together we pull up the heavy canvas top and begin to snap it onto the edges of the car. Then we see her. She's sauntering down the walkway like it's a catwalk. Murray has gone through a metamorphosis; this new butterfly looks like a Bay Area *Glam Queen*, not the tennis-playing heckler she used to be. Her once short, messy, light brown curls are all gone, and she slicks her curls back into a very large bun, mostly a hair piece. She's stunning—tall, with long tan legs like a racehorse, high cheekbones, oversized blue eyes and a saucy attitude. Her sunglasses are round, John Lennon style. She's wearing short frayed cut offs and a red top. She flashes her wide grin and says, "Welcome, Chickies."

Murray tells Rita her neighbor lady is out of town and suggests she use her covered garage. Rita wastes no time pulling her prized possession into security. We follow along on Murray's catwalk past a small lawn and around a building to see a well-weathered staircase belonging to the tall, old, very cool building whose basement is the home Murray shares with roommates.

Murray has prepared party snacks and a pasta salad. We lie around and listen to her talk about her new life and friends in *The City* as we nibble snacks and sip wine. I feel so grown up. Murray's cute blond roommate Kathy comes in through the front door carrying a bag of her recent purchases. She says she always shops when she's depressed. Out comes a bright yellow lace bra with matching bikini bottoms. Shock washes over me because I've never seen such magnificent underwear. I think to myself, She buys a fancy bra when she's feeling blue. Righteous! The four of us crack jokes, drink wine and Murray and Rita puff away. I can't help but think of my plain white cotton underpants and bra.

Soon I pull my camera out of the straw bag I'd bought in Avila Beach. It's a graduation gift from my mother. I begin to snap pictures of these fun friends whom I love so much. Kathy, the roommate, holds up her fancy yellow bra and I snap a picture. Now I'll have proof that I wasn't just dreaming.

Soon my artistic juices begin to flow. I suggest to Murray that she lie down on her very cool Indian carpet. Props are limited, so I tell her, "Now crawl under this dinner chair and put the side of your face in your hand." She stoops down, crawls under the chair and lies on her side, with her smiling face resting in her hand. I think it will be a fabulous shot, and I look forward to seeing it in a week or so when I get the roll of film developed. Posing for the camera is contagious, so the three of us run outside to take more shots. Murray smiles her winning smile in every pose.

Now we get really tricky-over-the-moon tricky. Rita and Murray run up the staircase and pose on the banister as if they're sliding down right toward the camera; they have their arms out and look like they're trying to keep their balance. I snap the picture and think we're onto something. I tell them I think the three of us will be famous someday.

Murray says, "Nah, that's just a feeling. Only you, Banana. You'll be a famous hairdresser and we'll be your agents."

Rita adds, "But Nana will only be famous in the red light district. *Miss Nana Gail* at your service."

"Yeah!" Murray finishes, "and Beehives half off!"

Rita and Murray have no boundaries or rules, and to them everything in life is cool. They are playful and mischievous and love to shock me with bad language. They tease, torture, basically pick on me, and I try to defend myself, but my laughter gets in the way. These playful routines have been ongoing since we were thirteen. We never have hassles or negative talk, just playful banter. Rita and Murray have given up on teaching me how to inhale, and they no longer engage in the battle to force me to say the F-word. I long ago realized the only way to win this war is to never say it. Ironically, not saying the F-word becomes my only weapon against these rambunctious harlots.

Many times, back in our hometown, specifically on very cold foggy nights, Murray and Rita roll down all the windows in Murray's Chevy. I'm in the backseat freezing. They tell me they'll roll up the window and turn on the heater if I say the F-word. I continue to curl up into a ball, using my brown corduroy jacket with a hood to keep from freezing to death, and state, "No, I won't say it!"

Finally they go ballistic and yell, "Why not?!"

I tell them, "Because it will break my mother's heart." I wait for their torrent of cuss words and they do flip out as I expect. Both turn in the front seat, put their arms over the edge and ask me why I refuse to say it. I stick to my guns because their reaction makes me smile inside, and finally they give up because they are cold themselves.

They say to each other, "Let's go home, she'll never say it."

I can hear them and it is so funny to me that now I've become invisible. Hearing them talk and give up tickles me inside. I bury my smile and know I have won.

The sun is going down in *The City*, and it's surprisingly cold. But still we unsnap the top of the Austin-Healey and climb in. I should have known I'd be put in the middle on a console the width of a candy bar. Rita zips up her nylon windbreaker and Murray puts on a wool plaid jacket with cuffs and a matching belt. I slip on my new jacket, a striped coat of white and tan shaggy fur. Murray laughs and tells Rita, "It looks like we've captured a big bear." Rita zooms up and over the streets.

Suddenly, Murray shouts, "Fuzz on the right!" And they both yell, "Nana, hide!" I slide down toward the stick shift, double over like a pretzel, and put my head in Murray's lap. She laughs and calls me a pervert. Murray spits out directions to Rita, and eventually tells me it's ok to sit up. We all agree to watch for *the heat*.

My butt scoots backward and I have to balance on the folded leather car top. I'm hanging on for my life as we zoom up and down the streets and over cable car tracks. There is nothing for me to grip except the rim of the windshield.

Rita drives back in the direction of *The Wharf* until we find Clown Alley. We park right in front so we can keep an eye on the Healey. Once inside, we grab some cheeseburgers, fries and sodas and sit there, right by the front window, eating and people watching for a long while. Rita buys a sweatshirt with a bold "Clown Alley" printed above the image of a happy crazy looking orange-haired clown. It's the perfect attire for Rita, who never wants to grow up. Marta, our smartest friend back home, says Rita suffers from arrested development. None of us knows what this means, but if Marta says it, then we agree.

The rest of the trip is a blur of too little sleep, too much eating, and just the right amount of shopping—not boring department store shopping, mind you. Our finest purchase comes after a jaunt over the Golden Gate Bridge to have lunch in Sausalito; we eat and watch sailboats. This groovy looking store is having a sidewalk sale and we spy matching pullovers hanging outside on a sale rack. Rita and I find two matching suede tops with criss cross leather lacing that beckon us to buy them. Rita's is chocolate brown, mine is tan.

On the end of our final day at Murray's place, Rita puts water on her curly hair to help control it, I backcomb my hair into a nice big bubble, then we both slip on our matching suede tops. Murray gives us instructions on how to get out of *The City*, and we wave goodbye, yelling last-minute one-liners and laughing as we drive away. Feeling very groovy in my new suede top, I slide down into the seat and Rita does what she does best: drive.

Easily we find a radio station and we turn up the music. We listen to John Sebastian, lead singer of the Loving Spoonfuls. *Oh yes, it is a wonderful day for a daydream.* We lift our long skinny arms up into the air and wave bye, and Rita roars around the corner.

She drives us back through *The City* and the Bay Area traffic. In 1964, traffic is beginning to get crowded, but Race-Car-Rita meanders us through the Sunday travelers, who also head for home.

We zoom back over the Pacheco Pass with our hair blowing in all directions. Rita stops at a little fruit stand called Casa de Fruta. We pick up some bananas, a bag of peanuts in the shell, and two juicy pears. I grab some paper towels and off we go. Rita hands me a cherry soda and she has a Coke. We eat, wipe our chins and try to keep our paper towels from blowing away.

We make our descent, and the air feels distinctly warmer. We snack, listen to music and make a mess. She asks if there is any place else I'd like to stop and I tell her, "If you see an orange juice stand, keep going." She looks over at me and we bust up laughing.

Rita changes the station to get better tunes out of Fresno. We cruise along listening to Roy Orbison and yell "Pretty Woman," and try to keep up with the song. Just as she turns onto the Highway, "Louie Louie" blasts on the radio. Rita yells to me over the wind, "I have no idea what they are singing about, do you know?"

I yell back, "I think he's singing about some chick named Louie Louie, oh, we gotta go now."

Home sweet home. Rita gets us through the maze of small towns and finally she turns left onto Olive Street and takes us straight to Coleman's. We order fries and milkshakes. Everyone knows we just pulled in from a long trip because our hair is standing up on end and we are wearing our groovy matching suede pullovers, which are way too hot for this time of year.

We go to the little drinking fountain and wipe our mouths and our sticky pear juice hands. After we eat, she drives down Olive and onto Main Street. We wave at locals cruising, then head home. The happiness of youth stays with me always.

If you're a true friend, you'll never
realize how weird your friends are
until you start to describe them to someone else.

The Roach Gang

THE WEEKEND BEFORE my highly anticipated freshman year of high school, two girl friends from a summer school typing class ask me to go with them to a party. Joanie and Trudy pick me up in a white Borgward. This party will change the course of my life and establish lifelong friendships.

There are so many kids at Norman's house! I never imagined such a gathering. His parents are out of town and kids are running in the front door and out the back, through the kitchen to the hallway, back and forth. Many are standing in the back yard while others walk into Norman's room, which is highly over-the-top decorated and was at one time his parents' disconnected garage with alley access.

The kitchen table seems to be a safe and inviting place. This kitchen is a short cut from the backyard to the living room. A guy walks up to the table and asks if he can join me. He introduces himself as Dennis, and he is the tallest man I've ever seen in my life. I look up and his legs go on forever. His hair is thick, wavy and very black, he has a prominent nose, and his eyes are close set, kind of like Lassie. We talk and I use every brain cell I can muster up to appear calm and mature. I'm still only thirteen, not yet fourteen until October. Dennis is going to be a junior this year. We watch the commotion and the high power insanity and we feel the intense energy whipping past us. He and I listen to the sounds of bedroom doors slamming and laughing and kids running down the hallway. Dennis suggests we eat some of Norman's mother's fruit from her nicely laid out display that beckons us from its place in the center of the table. I eat a banana, he crunches into an apple. We laugh and I jabber on about nothing, then we peek out the kitchen window towards Norman's room. I see Joanie, but not Trudy. There must be fifty kids in his small back yard, but Dennis and I decide to stay put, right there in the kitchen. I eat another banana, Dennis has a pear. We eat all the grapes too. Finally, after many hours and many laughs, Norman's mother's fruit plate is barren. Joanie and Trudy walk in from the backyard and decide to drag Main before heading home. I wave goodbye to my new tall dark handsome gentle friend.

The next day, Sunday, my sister tells me to get in the car; we need to go to the store. I grab a banana off the counter, run outside and jump in. While driving down Main Street, a car full of guys drives up next to us on the passenger side. It's my new friend Dennis, and he is driving his cousin's Chevy. He waves hello, and I wave back, but I still have a peeled banana in my hand. He laughs and says, "Look you guys, it's Banana." This nickname he yells out a car window stays with me all through high school. Even parents of friends begin to refer to me as Banana. The intersection is clear and my sister Bobbie takes off and so does Dennis, and as we accelerate, he yells back, "Meet me in the Cafeteria tomorrow."

My heart pounds as I walk into the high school cafeteria. How will I ever find him in such a huge room? I stand there, a low life freshman, searching for Dennis. Out of nowhere, he stands up and announces to a long line of students, "This is Banana." My knees knock together for a minute as he introduces Rita, Murray, Andrea, Norman, Marta, Jane, Tish, Betty Jo and a girl named Judy, just like me. This group of friends has been together since elementary school and some of them go back as far as Kindergarten. I wonder why I'm here.

I instantly recognize Murray because we met once on the school grounds at Bartlett Junior High. She was waiting for someone to pick her up and give her a ride home. She leaned on a post watching the street and shot me a snotty look. In a friendly voice I stated, "I know you. You're Peggy's sister," and Murray replied, "Yeah, so what."

I asked, "Are you in eighth grade?"

She responded, "What's it to ya," and walked off. Remembering this encounter I swallow and smile at her from across the lunch table; but she doesn't recognize me because I was just a pest on the school yard last spring.

Later on during the year, Murray and I start to have the beginnings of a friendship. When the bell rings for class changes, I walk down the hall wearing the new long full skirt Bobbie had sewn, and I have on a blouse and flats. Murray walks towards me through the crowd of kids, and yells, "Hey Banana, you've got a string hanging from your skirt." I look down and pause, look back up and she continues, "Oh, I'm sorry, that's your leg."

We both laugh, but I think to myself, one day I'll win this chick over, and she won't be so mean.

Later, during the winter months, she and I meet in a hallway and Murray has a puzzled look across her face. She asks, "Are you eating a banana or is that your nose?" Again she earns a huge laugh, but now I have her in my sights, and she'll beg for mercy one day.

Rita, on the other hand, sits there directly across from me day after day, eating her lunch while she sizes me up. She laughs with a smirk and spits out a few sarcastic remarks. She speaks softly, but her words are sharp and direct. Dennis laughs easily and speaks in his signature monotone voice; he delivers a very funny take on everything in life. Norman is more like a girl; he is gangly and his movements are fluid. His laughs are infectious, and he makes noises like a goose while he pinches girls' butts. He is hysterical and I'm told from the girls in my class that he dances like a professional. My dad observes, "He sure is light on his feet," but he says this to me in private. Another girl I meet in the lunch room is Burger, and boy is she gruff. I watch her but avoid making eye contact. When she belts out a laugh though, this makes me laugh and together we lose control and howl like two crazy people. Still, she and I have little connection and if we jump into her car, I always sit in the backseat.

Sometimes we drag Main; Joanie drives my '59 Opel. Norman, Dennis and the other Judy, who is also an upper classman, drive Norman's dad's 1960 Hillman station wagon. Rita, Marta, Murray and Andy are in GaGa's Go, and Trudy drives with her brother Bill in their parents' white German Borgward. Together we create a nerd parade. Then Joanie's dad buys a pink Edsel and my dad buys a Renault Dalphine and this seals the deal.

The Roach Gang

I ask Dennis to be my date to the King's Fling, a girl-ask-boy dance. I wear a full, lime green chiffon dress. We double date with Norman and his girlfriend Ellie, a cheerleader. Norman drives his dad's 1954 Coup de Ville Cadillac, maroon with double pointed tail lights. Finally we walk into the dance like two movie stars; Dennis just stands there and doesn't dance. Norman, on the other hand has enough energy and swing in his hips to dance with both me and Ellie. Dennis finally steps onto the dance floor a few times and we move slowly to the music, while Norman twirls circles all around us like a crazy egg beater. After the dance, Rita and Murray stop by my house on F Street and join us on the front porch. Mother steps out the front screen door with more Fritos and Eskimo Pies. Our house is one block off Olive Street, the other street that connects to Main Street—the two main drags. There we sit on the front porch and munch on treats. We watch cars cruise by bumper to bumper. They pass each other and honk, and we see arms waving out all four windows and hear yelling as they continue to cruise back and forth.

The cafeteria gang continues to meet at lunch time and others join in; it is a never ending supply of upper classmen and friends. Some days I walk with Rita and Murray across the street to Coleman's Drive-In for a quick lunch, and something different from what the cafeteria serves. We order chili poured over an open bag of Fritos, or hamburgers, fries and a coke for 35 cents. Then we walk down the unpaved alley and sit on garbage cans to eat our lunch. Despite the casual atmosphere, Rita's still aloof. I am friends with a guy who lands a job peeling potatoes for french fries, so sometimes we walk to the back room behind Coleman's and sit on cardboard boxes of unopened potatoes and eat lunch while Jerry peels. Potatoes, that is.

Marta drives Murray and Rita home after school in her 1954 tan Ford. One day they ask me to jump into her front seat. The first thing Marta says to me is, "Can you read?" She points toward the dashboard and taps her finger on the plastic note. I read the message she has stuck on her dashboard. It is made from a little machine that prints out letters. It reads, "This car runs on gas, not friendship." Like all the other passengers, I have to give Marta a dime or a quarter every time I hitch a ride.

My family moves back to the same house we lived in when I went to Belleview Elementary School in fifth grade. No more front porch, just a large field across the street.

Rita continues to eye me in the lunch room for about a month, and then one day my phone rings and it is Rita. She asks me what I'm doing and I reply, "Nothing, what are you doing?"

She replies, "Nothing." Awkward silence.

Then she asks me where I live and I answer, "Grand Avenue."

Rita states, "And you are a liar!"

This offends me so I ask her the obvious question, "Why would I lie about my address?" She demands that I describe my yard and house. I tell her that I live across the street from a big field and I can see Jimmy and Butch McLemore's house. My house is green with white trim. Rita orders me to step outside and stand on my front lawn. We plunk our receivers down at the same time. I step outside and look around and there is Rita, four houses down. We wave to each other and at the same time begin to walk toward each other, smiling. We meet smack dab in front of Leo's house.

Rita is smiling and I grin from ear to ear. I tell her about the girl who lives next door to her house. In fifth grade we were on her front porch playing jacks and she told me to look at my house. When I turned to look, she lifted up my sock, put a snail in there and smashed it. In slime shock I walked three houses back to my house crying. I go on to tell Rita that my dad saw me walk past our living room window, he ran outside, scooped me up and carried me in his arms and put me on my bed. He took off my sock and called my mother, who wiped the gick off my foot. Rita asks me if the girl's name is Diana, and I nod yes. We look at each other and we know instantly what we have to do.

The next weekend we carve our initials into Diane's large sycamore tree that sits very close to Rita's cinder block fence; it's an easy target.

R. S.
+
J. G.

Then Rita places a sprinkler in Diana's back porch and turns on the hose. We skin our knees climbing up and over the cinder blocks' dried goops of concrete. We jump into her Grandma's car, which we call *GaGa's Go*, and leave the scene of the crime. Rita is just fourteen years old so we only drive down Grand Avenue to the Village Market and buy some peanuts. Our mission of retribution towards the bully lasts about one year. Diana tries to avoid making eye contact with us, but we take great joy in staring her down and giving her the evil eye.

Rita tells me an interesting story as we chug along in GaGa's Go. When Rita moved in, the bully next door warned Rita to stay away from me. She told Rita, "There is a girl who lives just down the street and you need to stay away from this girl. Her name is Judi, and Judi is big trouble." That girl is me, and Rita only knows me as Banana, so she never puts two and two together. All the times we meet in the cafeteria she never connects the two names. Rita and I have a good laugh about the bully's warning. It's obvious Diana knew that if I met Rita, one day I'd tell her about the snail squishing incident. And there's another joke: Rita is two times more trouble than Diana could ever imagine.

Halloween is here. Rita and I walk to the local VFW Hall where a party is going on. We each carry a concealed bar of soap in our pocket and we begin to draw designs on car windows. She draws scary faces and the outline of the bird (the finger, not a sparrow), and I write my name in lovely serif. In a small town like Porterville, it takes no time at all for my parents to hear about the soap creativity, and I am forced to admit to soaping car windows. Rita's name is never mentioned.

Life continues with my new friend and neighbor. We meet every day in the cafeteria, eat lunch across from each other, and always sit with the same people. All of the gang at our long table except me attended Roach elementary school together, and this creates a tight bond no one can penetrate. They continue to talk about elementary school antics and Roach Jokes, which leaves me out of the loop. Yes, the elementary school is Roach, located on Roach Avenue. I wonder who names a school or a street *Roach*? I attended Olive Street School, then Belleview School and I think these are pretty names.

Andy tells a story over the lunch table one afternoon. She and her gang of friends are about 11 years old. She says that she, Murray, Marta and Rita went out one night to prowl around and look for mischief. They see some ladies playing cards, so they sneak around to the backyard to an enclosed porch. The young girls get a hose, uncoil it, and

Rita and Murray put it inside the screened in porch. Rita twists a sprinkler head on the ladies' own hose, and either Andy or Murray turns the water on full blast and the girls take off. Marta is the lookout stationed at the front of the house, but she fails to notice the people across the street who are sitting on their front porch in the dark, facing her.

A man yells, "Hey, what are you kids doing over there?" and Marta yells, "Running!"

Rita, Murray, Andy and Marta are used to being mischievous. Sometimes they collect dog poop, put it into paper bags, set the bags on someone's porch, light them on fire, ring the doorbell and run.

There is a photo I've seen many times over the years. This photo includes Murray, Rita, Andy and Marta. These mischievous girls, who look to be about twelve, are at Rita's house; she is having a slumber party. The pranksters have on their pajamas, which they layer with their clothes over the top. GaGa snaps this great picture, with the slumber partiers each holding and chugging Root Beer.
Then, when GaGa is out of sight, the four girls climb up on the roof. Oh how I wish I'd gone to Roach Avenue School with these wild girls.

1960—Andy to the Rescue

My sister bought a white Impala with a large wide trunk and fins, and I inherited her Opel Cadet, 1959. I am only fourteen, and untrained, so I put the Opel into first gear, the only gear I know, and chug down the back streets to Andy's house, who is sixteen. She drives us to the roller skating rink or bowling alley, or to Coleman's, and we look for friends. It is so much fun to have wheels and be downtown with all the other kids. Andy and I meet up with Dennis and he jumps in with us and we play chase and ditch with the out-of-towners. He drives the Opel up and over and around the only hill in town. Off we go into the countryside, driving fast with only the sound of pipes. Dennis drives, or sometimes Rita, Murray or Andy will take the wheel. It is fun because the Opel is fast and has three inch glass packed pipes that pop multiple times with every down shift. The chasers can hear us, but never find us.

One night Andy and I get so bored she pushes in the electric lighter and smashes it on my leg. Boy that hurt. I push it back in and when it pops out, I smash it on her face, on her cheekbone. We both scream and laugh out of pain. We are hurting and we have no idea why we are doing such a stupid thing to each other. Andy drives herself home and I chug my way back to Grand Avenue. We doctor our circles of burnt flesh and continue to be friends.

Andy is real cute. She is short, and her hair is a soft red and is cut into a bubble. Her face has a nice sprinkle of freckles, and when she laughs her eyes go shut and her whole face and body seem to giggle. Marta has red hair too, but her hair is orange flame red and her light blue eyes can pierce a hole right through you. Murray, with her big blue eyes and messy light brown hair, always has this look on her face: the look of someone who is thinking of a smug joke. She also looks as if she is ready to pounce with enjoyment.

Some nights Rita suggests we cruise Main Street in her Grandma's car, just for kicks. GaGa's car is a 1950 blue Dodge that has a fluid drive transmission. Murray and I jump into GaGa's Go with Rita behind the wheel. She starts the engine and we move slowly forward while the car chugs us down the dark street alongside her house. Then, just before we reach the corner, the car automatically lurches into second gear causing our heads snap back. We have more fun in GaGa's Go than in any other car. The seats are itchy nylon and it feels like we are back in another time. It is especially fun when we take off from a stop sign, rumble, wait, and prepare for a head snap, as the fluid transmission goes into second gear.

Everyone who runs with Rita has an episode in GaGa's Go. Sometimes she asks her grandma to drive her to the store. She says, "No turn right. No not right, GaGa. I said left. Now take a quick right. No not right, I said left." Rita yells, "GaGa, pay attention! Now go straight. No, not that way, this way." GaGa acts flabbergasted and upset, but it is all a well-rehearsed act, as she loves Rita and enjoys her pranks, which never ease up.

Rita and Murray are on the high school tennis team and I am on the swim team, so naturally we all have short hair. One night, bored out of our gourd, we slick our hair back and put shoe polish on it to make it dark. The result is super shiny Elvis hair. We accentuate this look by pulling more hairs forward that hang on our foreheads, like the guys who wear waterfalls. We slip on black jackets and Rita wears a white t-shirt and puts a pack of cigarettes in her sleeve then rolls the sleeve up and over the pack. We resemble greasy good for nothin' hoodlums. Off we go in GaGa's Go to look for trouble. No one will honk at us or wave, so we slide down deeper into the seats to look as bad and dangerous as we can. Then we spot our targets: two cousins who are cheerleaders who dress in full skirts and nylons and little high heel pumps to school every day. These cousins have poise and class, and their hair is never out of place—large bubbles with a perfect flip on the bottom. They are both super nice, and we like them a lot, but we also believe they will be easy to scare.

Murray is our driver, I'm in the back seat sitting low so only the top of my greasy hair and sunglasses are visible. Rita rides shotgun with her arm hanging out the window to expose the outline of her pack of Chesterfields. The cousins see us watching them and they scream, then they drive off to a side street. Murray follows, keeping a good distance behind them, like a stalker. We see their tail lights turn right and take a short cut as they try to ditch us. But this is our town too, so Murray cuts them off at the end of the street. Rita yells at them, "Where's the fire?" They drive quickly back downtown for safety and we follow, honking and yelling, "Pull over! Let's party," and "Hey good lookin'!" Finally after an hour of following and cutting them off, the girls head towards one of their homes. Murray floor boards it and drives like a race car driver in GaGa's car and arrives before they do. She parks across the street in a secured location under the shade of a huge tree that shadows us from the exposing moon light. We wait and talk and decide to scare them just one more time then drive off. Finally we see headlights coming down the street, and hear their car as they come around the curve of upscale homes.

They pull into her parents' driveway and we *hoods* watch as they lock the car doors, look around and step onto the lawn. Just then, Murray pulls on the headlights. The cousins quickly look toward the car lights, and Murray yells, "Nice house!"

They scream and run across the remaining few feet of manicured lawn and Rita yells, "Want an Oly?"

While they try to unlock the front door, a man comes to the door and the girls run past him to safety. We sit there and watch them peek out the window. The man, one of the girls' fathers, stands there watching us and Murray lays rubber and peels out. Well, we actually wait for the car to lurch into second gear, and then she peels out. We head back to Rita's house and wash out the grease and shoe polish from our hair using laundry detergent.

On Monday morning, we wait for Murray to skid around the corner in her pink and gray '55 Chevy; she's late as usual, we jump into her car all grumpy. There is already gossip at school about the hoods that were in town Saturday night. Everyone in our school hears about these three punks stalking girls and dragging Main, but *Elvis*, *James Dean* and *Conway Twitty* are never seen again.

1962

A high school graduation gift from Mombo, Rita's mom, to Andy is inviting her to go on a road trip with her and Rita through Yellowstone National Park. They watch Old Faithful and hunt for a good place to camp. Andy tells us that while camping or driving, Mombo likes to play a game of rhymes: bear/care, pine/sign, snake/rake, cone/bone and so on. As they eat dinner over an open fire they continue to rhyme into nightfall. Then they fetch water from a creek, brush their teeth and crawl into their sleeping bags and wait for sleep to take over. It is a once in a lifetime trip and Andy recalls the location Mombo chooses is in the middle of Yellowstone National Park and they sleep without a tent. Andy does not sleep. She is awake all night preparing to be eaten alive by a bear or something worse.

The next morning Marie fixes the girls breakfast, and they clean and pack up. Marie drives the girls west, towards Seattle, to visit the 1962 Seattle World's Fair. For the trip, Marie surprises them with extra-long cigarette holders. Andy and Rita sit in the backseat and puff away, with their cigarettes in holders like movie stars, and they practice blowing smoke rings. All the while Andy keeps thinking, "My mother would kill me if she knew what I'm up to." When they return home and the end of summer comes, Andy moves out of town to attend college. I am already out of town for the summer and Andy and I don't cross paths again for many years.

1963

Tonight Rita and Murray will graduate from high school and attend the all night graduation party. Rita invites Dennis, who graduated a year ahead of them, to join her and Murray. He happily joins them and their celebration. First they drive around town, then up to Scenic Heights where they park and drink cherry sloe gin. Finally the threesome attends their all night grad party at the looming prestigious Elks Hall facing Main Street. Dennis stands in the food line and eats many bowls of macaroni salad. Later in the evening he is found passed out in the men's room, in a stall. Someone takes him outside and down the concrete steps just as Norman and his girlfriend cruise by. They get Dennis into the car and continue to drag Main, unaware that inside Dennis, the cherry sloe gin and macaroni aren't mixing well; he sticks his head out the window to get some air. Norman sees Burger drive by. He waves her down and asks her to take Dennis far away. They pull into the closed gas station located next door to the Elks Club to make the switch. Burger takes him, all six-foot-six of him, and drags him into the men's room and shuts the door. Dennis enjoys the cold concrete floor and continues to barf. This story is hazy due to the fact that all players are inebriated. Someone finds Dennis and rescues him. He is passed out, and is pulled by his feet out into the parking lot, where someone takes him to Norman's house and leaves him on the front lawn. The bathroom is a total mess.

Norman is still trying to impress his date and continues to cruise back and forth downtown in his 1960 Cadillac Seville Sedan. Ellie sits close to Norman as they cruise and wave to everyone, then he parks at Coleman's to get some sodas. Norman gets out and walks around to the passenger's side to help Ellie out of the car and sees Dennis' gift. Pink macaroni is stuck to the side of his car, all the way from the passenger door to the back of those large pointed fins. Norman slams the car door, jumps in and drives as fast he can back to his house to hose off his car and wipe away the evidence. He is surprised to see Dennis passed out on his lawn. Rita and Murray finally emerge from the Elks Club at sunrise, and somehow make it home. I suspect Burger, the angel of mercy, helps them too.

This day of graduation and intense partying is the kick off for a summer I will miss. It's also the day I drive my mother in my Corvair and follow my dad to Lakeport. He has taken a job advancement and I will complete my senior year 400 miles away to the north, by a huge lake. Our house on Grand Avenue is for sale.

While I'm in town, our gang spends many evenings at Mickey and Larry's, the only couple in our group of friends. Mickey likes to cook and we enjoy many wonderful taco feeds with rice, refried beans and casseroles. Countless evenings are spent at Mickey and Larry's house, but I don't recall ever bringing food even once. It just never occurs to us to help. The good news is our gang has a place to convene, eat, visit and play Clue. I drive back and forth from Lakeport most weekends.

One of our favorite games is Clue. Mickey passes around a bowl with pieces of paper, and we each pick one. We read what we unfold to see if we are witnesses, a victim, or the murderer. Someone else is the investigator, who flicks off the lights. We wait five minutes while we mill around the house, then the lights flick back on. The victim lies on the floor, or draped across a chair, and waits for us to find the murderer. When the investigator asks, "Where were you standing?" everyone has to stop in their tracks, not move, and one by one answer his probing questions.

One evening while sitting around, we friends begin to play a game of telling each other what type of flower we are, or what type of animal. I guess it is a safe way of letting each other know what we really feel without getting too mushy. Someone describes me as a daisy. Rita is a rose; pretty to look at but it has thorns.

IT IS ONE OF THE BLESSINGS OF OLD FRIENDS THAT YOU CAN AFFORD TO BE STUPID WITH THEM.

Ralph Waldo Emerson

Hag Hollow

RITA'S MOTHER, whom she fondly refers to as Mozie, has a good friend Liz. They met while working together at the local Library. They seem to be the same type of person. They both enjoy a good smoke, a good book, and a good stiff drink after work. Somewhere along the line, Marie and Liz decide to pool their resources and buy a cabin up in Camp Nelson.

You can reach Camp Nelson, which is a quaint little village with a huge impressive lodge, in about forty-five minutes. The drive up into the mountains is a drive east from Porterville through the small mountain town of Springville, then up a long treacherous winding road. But it's worth the view when the miracle of Ponderosa Pines and huge Sequoias begins to appear. Generations of cabins are sprinkled about the village. The coffee shop and a little grocery store are across the street from the lodge. When you step out of your car, the smell of cedar and pine is overwhelming and all you want to do is lie in a hammock between two redwoods and fall asleep.

At Camp Nelson you can cook in your cabin or you can grab a bite to eat at the coffee shop, then you can venture out into the cool mountain air. The mammoth lodge comes alive on weekends with great Rock and Roll or Blue Grass bands or any variety of entertainers.

We call the cabin Hag Hallow. Who names a cabin Hag Hallow? Marie and Liz, that's who. The name is dark just like the cabin. It always seems dark there because the shadows of the branches of the tall pines encase the little cabin and only allow occasional flashes of sun light to reach it. The cabin, located over the second mountain past Camp Nelson, is on a semi private, slightly winding road to nowhere. Marie and Liz pull into their dirt driveway every Friday night and enter another world—the world of Hag Hollow.

Their cabin is essentially one large room with a pop out area that provides a private bathroom and storage. Couches, wingback chairs, ottomans, and twin beds line the walls, and there's a throw rug in the center. Various cubbies around the room contain rolled up sleeping bags. The back and sides of the cabin have a deck that offers a great view. When you stand on the deck and look outward, the sight of amazing mountains never ends. When you look down, your eyes find long, uneven slopes full of tall grass, misshapen boulders, sparse pine trees, and some long-ago rotted fallen branches. If you scour the scene long enough, you'll catch a glimpse of water. A nice little winding creek provides all kinds of activity; it's a place for fishing, tossing skippers, exploring, or just soaking your feet.

But by far the best part of Hag Hollow is my dear friend Rita, who has a key. And permission.

The road to Hag Hollow—just like its story—is a very long and winding one. Let's back track.

Here is a cheat sheet for the reader: Marie, Mozie and Mombo are one and the same person. Rita refers to her mother, Marie, as Mozie. We friends know her as Mombo. Ok, here goes the story of Hag Hollow.

In the mid 1940s Marie lives in Santa Monica and as luck would have it, she meets and marries Jimmy. Jimmy works as a machinist for a National Aviation Company called Norton. Jimmy's first wife was killed in an automobile accident seven years prior, when their son Bill was just three.

Jimmy's talent and expertise leads him to work on the B-25 bomb during World War II. A mechanical genius, he carefully and painstakingly works on a design that leads him to build the first bomb that is launched off a naval carrier towards its intended target, Japan. He designs the bomb viewer by using black widow spider cross hairs to secure an accurate target.

While Marie and Jimmy are together in Santa Monica, they sometimes drive to Los Angeles to sit in on a talk or game show. One day, Jimmy applies and is accepted as a guest on the weekly show *Truth or Consequences* with the famous host Ralph Edwards. Jimmy misses the question and has to take the Consequence.

Jimmy meets a crew in the very wealthy section of Beverly Hills and sets up a tri pod right on someone's yard to survey for a job. Many of the wealthy home owners walk outside to ask him what he is doing in their gated community and inform him he is standing on private property. He explains to them that he works for the Pacific Railroad and he is surveying the street and lawns to prepare for the train tracks that will run through this neighborhood. Naturally the affluent residents begin to yell and cuss at him, and try to run him off. The camera crew steps out of hiding in the bushes, and everyone is surprised and thrilled to be on a taping of *Truth or Consequences*.

Jimmy and his new wife Marie eventually move. The war is over and his job no longer exists. They pack up youngster Bill and baby Rita, and leave Santa Monica for the lush lands of Central California. They choose the small town of Strathmore, which consists mostly of citrus and other fruit trees, decorative palms, scattered barns and horse arenas. Strathmore sits between Porterville and Lindsay. Jimmy purchases a red brick house with lots of style in the architecture.

Young Bill is transferred from his upscale Santa Monica school to attend a new school in Strathmore where there are only five kids, of all ages, herded into one classroom. Marie takes a job in the credit department for Montgomery Wards in Porterville, the nearest town, and Jimmy works for Lindsay Ripe Olive, the largest olive grower in the world. When Rita is five years old, she is enrolled at Roach Elementary School, in Porterville.

Marie buys a palomino horse and her sister Margaret, who lives in Porterville, buys some expensive special breeds and keeps them on Marie's property. Jimmy has a work area inside the barn where he tinkers and invents on his days off. Marie and Margaret begin to make jellies and jams to sell on the roadside of the busy Hwy 65. They name their business *Simpson's Kitchen*.

Jimmy drives the shaker for Lindsay Ripe Olive, and in his spare time in his barn, he invents a way to efficiently shake the olives off the trees without causing damage. Then, as rumor has it (and this comes from reliable sources—Marie, Rita and Bill), Jimmy, in his beloved workshop, invents the olive pitter. He will lose his job if he takes any credit for his masterful invention so, being a family man, he makes the choice to take a large lump sum of money instead of the patent. This is how life is in the lean days after the war.

Rita and her brother Bill are ten years apart in age and, as Bill explains, their relationship as brother and sister is more like ships passing in the night. When Rita is old enough to carry on a conversation, Bill is away at college, then marries and moves to the Bay Area. Each child essentially is raised as an only child.

People say Jimmy looks like the famous comedian Bob Hope, and acts like him too. They describe him as the guy with a dry sense of humor who makes everyone laugh. Marie sports a salty wicked sense of humor with a very flat dry delivery. Bill and Rita naturally inherit the gift of a good one liner as they mature, and they each see the world as an opportunity to state the obvious with a quick salty delivery.

One day, just like always, Jimmy comes home from work and parks under the same big shade tree he does every day. He walks down the long sidewalk toward the front door of their tidy red brick house and collapses from a massive heart attack. He dies where he falls, on the path to his front door. Rita is ten years old, and possibly a witness to this; Bill is twenty years old and away at college.

After a few years, Marie reluctantly sells the house, acreage and horses, and moves to Porterville. This move proves to be the best choice for Marie, and more especially for her pre-teen daughter.

Marie takes a job as a librarian at the Porterville City Library, and the tables start to turn. Marie buys a house that is secure, well built, and located on a shady corner lot on Grand Avenue. Marie also moves her mother in to watch over Rita and the household duties. When GaGa arrives, the stable household turns into a highly stimulated stable household of long running practical jokes—a home full of antics and music.

Marie and Liz, both librarians, team up as best friends and business partners. With the money from the sale of her horses, Marie buys a dirt bike; Liz buys one also. They mount the bikes to the back of their small truck and off they go on weekends. The backs of their dirt bikes are piled high with sleeping bags and food. During this time is the birth of Hag Hollow.

Liz and Marie drive up to their cabin every Friday night. On Saturdays they take long rides on their dirt bikes high up into the mountains.

Without fail, eventually they run into a camp of hunters who like to sit around and talk to them about their boring marriages and dead deer. I'm certain Marie and Liz leave them in a cloud of dust. They love this part of their lives: riding dirt bikes up the winding roads and into the pines with shear rock drop offs, or following beautiful rivers that crisscross and snake through the wilderness.

Many of the cabins are old family inheritances—homes to retirees, and some are new, with all the trimmings. From Hag Hollow it is a long drive back to the small market. Good sense is, if you need groceries and you don't want to eat in a café, all your needs have to be brought up with you on Friday nights.

Back at Hag Hollow, the only sounds in the area are birds singing and water bubbling over the rocks down the creek. It's a lovely stress-free environment for two friends who are both hard working mothers and full time librarians.

Hag Hollow is well known in the area because of its name and the crude painted sign on gnarly wood that sits right on the side of the road. The cabin is located on Slate Mountain just behind the first mountain, which is the main part of town. This is their getaway from the public library and the never-ending questions from readers they deal with on a daily, hourly basis. It's a wonderful chance to rest, have a good stiff drink and go for miles on their dirt bikes.

Camp Nelson

Resting at Hag Hollow, Liz and Marie like to smoke and drink and tell tall tales with explicit adjectives and storylines, while Marie keeps a cigarette hanging out the corner of her mouth like a sexy thug. I think Mombo is a very pretty lady. She's tiny, with short white wavy hair she parts on one side, and she lets her natural wave flow backwards. She also has a tight smile, and a personality with a smirk to go with it. But Liz, well she scares me to death. She looks stern, dry and has a slight hook nose and large eyes. She uses her vocabulary to her advantage. Everyone loves Liz, but I shy away from her and suspect she likes to intimidate unsuspecting kids. She has a way about her that implies: no shenanigans. She is smart, poised and very clever.

Liz is the mother to three. Her oldest son goes by his nickname, Bookie, and she has a daughter Ann, and another son Edward. Liz's kids are like family to Rita. They adore their mother, which makes me realize that my impression of Liz is that of an unaware kid who is used to a very quiet gentle mother. Just one look of acceptance or a nod from Liz makes me feel like a complete and worthwhile human being.

Mombo is pretty, with a little pink across her nose from sun or drink, but she is an adult Tom Boy, kind of like a girl guy. I tread lightly, as I have a natural fear of her. I think it is because of her keen mind and my built-in intuition that I am no match to her banter. Some days when I hang out at Rita's, I like to clean up her mother's discarded cigarette butts. The thick crystal ashtray on a stand made of gold art deco design calls me from Mombo's bedroom. I dump out the butts, wash the heavy thick glass with soap and water, and happily polish it with a cloth. She notices the clean ashtray one afternoon and demands, "Who keeps dumping my butts and washing the ashtray?"

I step into her room and say, "I did it, Mombo."

She looks at me with that smirk and says, "So, Banana, I see you are a perfectionist."

I shrug my shoulders and mumble, "I guess so." This confrontation chills me to the bone, just to have a conversation with her.

She smirks, then informs me she needs to pick up a butt now and then. "So let's not toss my butts out anymore, shall we?"

When we are alone, Rita smiles at me and says, "That'll teach you."

Later on, as I grow older, Mombo and I have many talks about grammar, and about my long legs and long stride and the art of walking on hard wood floors. She tells me to try and step more lightly, and to walk like a lady, not an elephant. Then she smiles. She also suggests that I push my tooth back in place when I go to sleep at night. I argue that when you fall asleep so will your finger. She takes her finger and pushes it on her tooth and says, "Like this. Push it all the time and it will go back into place."

One day, for no reason, Mombo thanks me for continuing to watch over her butts. This is the beginning of my admiration that sprouts out of fear. I love it when she smiles. I also love it that she takes an interest in me.

When Liz was living and working in Los Angeles, she was the personal secretary for the actress Bette Davis. I have no idea how long she held this position or why she left to move to the central valley, except that she probably needed to be in a smaller town to raise her children. I suppose she wanted a more rural life for them, the same reason Marie made decisions concerning Rita.

During the summer of 1962, actress Bette Davis comes to our little town of Porterville to visit Liz. They go to Gang Sue's Chinese restaurant and eat lunch in the Ming room. Also invited to this magical luncheon are Marie, Rita and Rita's two pals from elementary school, Marta and Murray.

Marta has fiery copper color hair, cut into a fluffy bubble, and light blue eyes, and she likes to remind people she has a temper to go along with her red hair. Marta is quiet, attentive and when she speaks, you listen. This is a good choice for this luncheon guest. Murray is very cool and confident, also a good idea. Rita, Marta and Murray are in awe to be sitting next to this famous actress. In all their glory, in the presence of such a huge icon and in our small town, Rita, Marta and Murray have lunch with Bette Davis, and right under our nose! Murray recalls this luncheon with fondness. She doesn't remember any of them uttering one word. Bette Davis must have put a spell on the pranksters and shut them down. One day I ask Murray why I wasn't invited and she says, "Because you were living in Oakland for the summer, Chickie, and I hate to add salt to the wound Banana, but you missed having lunch with Bette Davis!" She grins. Ugh, she gets me again. Liz and Bette Davis remain lifelong friends.

Rita spends many evenings and weekends with her Mozie when they visit Liz's house and her three children. She is the youngest kid when visiting them. This is why she is so ornery and full of pranks; it's all for attention. She wants her mother to notice her. Marie is aware of Rita and enjoys her spirited nature, but she is also very busy, working all of the time then hot footing it up to Hag Hollow. Rita's mind never stops. She is either playing cards or learning how to bet on a black jack hand. She plays the piano, plays with her cats and drives all over the state. Sometimes I wonder if she ever just lies on her bed and thinks—like—contemplates life.

Hag Hollow fills our heads with many memories of the fearless Rita. On a weekend of trust from Mombo, we pack in lots of canned foods, packages of Lipton soup, and lots of sodas. Bags of potato chips, Frito's, cans of chili and hot chocolate are there for our pleasure. We spend most of our summer days running down the hillside to the creek and we search for the perfect flat rock for tossing skippers.

In the winter we use pieces of cardboard or garbage can lids and slide down the hill towards the freezing water. We laugh like wild animals, and drag a hurt friend back up to the cabin. We chase each other, take long walks, smoke, and build toasty fires. Nighttime parties are games of checkers, or we play Scrabble. But the night usually ends up with a good game of Black Jack. Rita loves to gamble. If someone curls up and falls asleep, for sure Rita will put pepper under their nose.

Some members of the Hag Hollow gang continue to caravan up to the cabin and raise hell. Others arrive at different times to get away from parents and party. Hag Hollow's minimal square footage makes the guest list smaller than we'd like. There are always plenty of blankets and flashlights though, so it's lots of fun to run outside and play hide and seek in the pitch black forest.

Sometimes Dennis and Norman drive up the mountain in Norman's '57 Chevy Bel Air after a Saturday night dance in town. When they slowly drive in close and park, they like to make noises to sound like a bird in the rain forest, then they claw the front door to scare us. Murray and Rita finally see Norman's car in the shadows and yell, "The police are on their way!" When they step in, Hag Hollow comes alive with new sounds, stories and laughter—the cabin is full of life.

Another time, Dennis and Norman drive up for a few days. Dennis pulls his parents' trailer using his '56 Chevy pickup truck. They find a camp spot, settle in, and hike to Hag Hollow to see Rita, Murray and Marta. All day they hang out, eat and play cards. They realize they've overstayed the curfew of the camp site and now they're locked out with a chain across the posts. The five card sharks hike in the dark with flashlights through the forest until they find the trailer. Rita darts off into the night and short cuts to the trailer park to get there ahead of the others. She lets herself in with the key Dennis handed over to her, and is inside the trailer. She locks the door behind her and begins to remove all the labels off the tin can goods. When she is finished, she stacks them back into the cabinet and stuffs the labels into her jacket pocket. Her friends arrive and she lets them in with a smile. "Welcome!" she says, and hands the keys back to Dennis. They decide to meet there for lunch the next day.

Dennis puts a pan on the burner and opens up the small pantry above; there he sees a bunch of tin cans without labels. He knows immediately it's the work of Rita. Dennis stands and stares and has no idea what he might open; could be beans, maybe corn, or pineapple. This is a typical calling card from Rita; he pictures her smirking to herself all the way back to Hag Hollow.

One time, Rita hurt her leg running down the hill in the snow. Burger is a witness but she is of no help because she lets out a belly laugh and just watches Rita hopping along. More laughter comes along when Rita tries to lift her hurt leg and get it over a fence. We are young and immune to pain. Finally we gather enough brain cells and realize she is badly hurt and we carry her back up the hill to wrap her leg with an ace bandage. When an injury occurs, I recede from the medical care and leave it to the others. My job is to stare out over the deck and keep an eye out for wild life and dangerous animals. Rita recovers with the aid of a good stiff drink and a homemade splint.

"How does this happen?" Andy says, once the girls are stranded up at Hag Hollow without a ride home. They hike to a neighbor, who gives them a ride to the Camp Nelson grocery store, where they borrow the telephone. Three tries finally land a friend who agrees to help; it's Bookie, Liz's oldest son. He drops whatever he is doing and drives up immediately to taxi the girls back down the mountain.

The girls jump into his Cadillac La Salle, and he takes them back to the cabin to retrieve all of their things and lock up the cabin properly. They start down the winding mountain road with sheer drop offs. Bookie then, for some crazy reason, puts his huge tub of a car in neutral and lets it glide its way down the mountain. He is showing off, I suspect for Andy. Rita gets madder than a wet hen. Murray yells at him to stop being an ass wipe and to start the engine. Andy is scared speechless, begs him to start the engine and says the steering might lock up. Rita begins to cuss him out, but he ignores their pleas and continues to *coast* down the winding road. He finally turns on the engine and no one speaks to him all the way down the hill. They gather their things and slam the car doors.

On one of our last days at the cabin, Rita is hungry and there is no food, so she digs around in the cabinets, cusses then goes to the fridge. There she finds some raw sausage. Marta and Murray try to warn her, but she likes to be daring and shock people. Despite their warnings not to eat it, Rita gobbles down two sausages anyway. Rita spends the next few hours barfing and heaving her guts up, then she has a wonderful time serenading us with her rendition of "the dry heaves."

Hag Hollow is the place to be. Rita drives up to Camp Nelson after work on a Friday night; she always drives past a local camp spot north of Springville named Coffee Camp. She drives by the camp ground late at night on purpose. When she roars down the road, she tosses fire crackers out of her Austin-Healy to scare and wake up the campers, then she zooms into the night. None of us would do this, but Rita doesn't know the difference between being naughty and being funny. I suspect she pulls over, lights the ends, takes off like a bat out of hell, and tosses. She never has anyone to get after her; her Mother is busy with her social life and GaGa is certainly out of the loop. If anyone was camping at Coffee Camp and remembers the sounds of multiple and rapid gun fire, it was Rita. No worries.

On a Friday night Rita drives alone to Hag Hollow to do work on the cabin. She cleans and moves things around, and relaxes. I finish work on Saturday about three o'clock and meet her there to have dinner. The next day, we have a great day hiking around the neighborhood, then come back and Rita tries to teach me how to play five card draw. By dusk we decide to caravan back down the winding road. Rita takes off, but my VW decides to play dead. Worry sets in as the sun threatens to set behind the sharp mountain peak. In about ten minutes I hear the familiar roar coming closer around the many curves. She's come back to check on my whereabouts. Rita digs into her glove box, finds a pencil and begins to work on the engine while I hold the flash light. Seems like forever, but in about twenty minutes sweet Rita fixes the problem. The bug starts up with its familiar sewing machine hum.

Rita tells me she'll drive ahead and says for me to follow so her lights can lead the way. She notes that we need to hurry because it's starting to get chilly. She drives off. I back out and slowly drive down the winding narrow roads until I reach Camp Nelson. Within minutes I'm out of town and humming along down the hill. I look over at the steep cliffs and see the moon's reflection on the rock walls. I lean in to the dashboard and search for a radio station, which is tedious business as I listen and slowly turn the knob. Finally a station comes in and great music fills my little bug. I continue to follow Rita down the hill, singing along with Simon and Garfunkel to Homeward Bound, a perfect song. With caution I steer my Bug safely down the steep mountain road, and don't see Rita's lights.

I hum through Springville and buzz on down towards our town. The winding road begins to even out, and finally I make it to Olive Street. I can't find Rita anywhere, so I drive by her house, drive past five bars, then by Judy (Burger) Weisenburger's house, my mother's house, Judy Annestad's house, and Norman's house, then back downtown and cruise Main Street to Olive Street and back again. She is nowhere. Then, after thirty minutes of driving aimlessly in circles, I feel tired and home beckons me. Just as I turn left to head home, there is Rita roaring up behind me. I pull over and she parks. She walks towards the back of my VW Bug.

Rita squats on the curb, I reach across and roll down the window. She looks inside my passenger window and she has no smile or smirk. She begins to tell me that her car overheated halfway down the mountain. She says she had to pull over to the only safe place, which is a tiny, thin strip of earth under a piece of hanging rock, and wait. Rita continues on, "I see your car lights coming around a few turns and I look up towards the mountain and see you." She goes on, "I wave my arms and jump up and down, crossing my arms. You drive right past me and it appears to me that you are singing!" She tells me that she assumes I'll pull over at some point, but instead she watches as the little VW tail lights continue on down the hill, curve after curve.

I feel so bad, as bad as a good friend can feel. Rita continues to go off on me. "I fix your car with a God damned pencil, and how do you thank me?" Deep breath, "You roar off into the sunset, that's what. You leave me to freeze in the f***ing dark!"

She stands up and walks back to her car while I yell, "I'm sorry, I didn't see you." She plops down and slams her car door. The usually heartwarming roar of her engine revs up and she flips a U-turn and roars off without a wave.

The next day, late morning, I drive from mother's house to Rita's. I open the creaky back door, and she is standing right there in the kitchen. Rita looks at me and stares. She walks straight over to the counter, drops two pieces of bread into the toaster, looks straight back at me with no expression and flatly asks, "Butter, Nana?"

Rita then sits down at her grand piano and plays "Cast Your Fate to the Wind," her signature piece. When her song is over she hits all the keys at once with the palms of her hands. We crunch on buttered toast with jam, jump into her car, and drive around town to find friends. Nothing is ever said about our misadventure. This will be the one and only time Rita is ever angry with me.

This is also the last time we are at Hag Hollow. Marie and Liz put their cabin up for sale. Everything seems to change, no matter how much we want our world to stay the same.

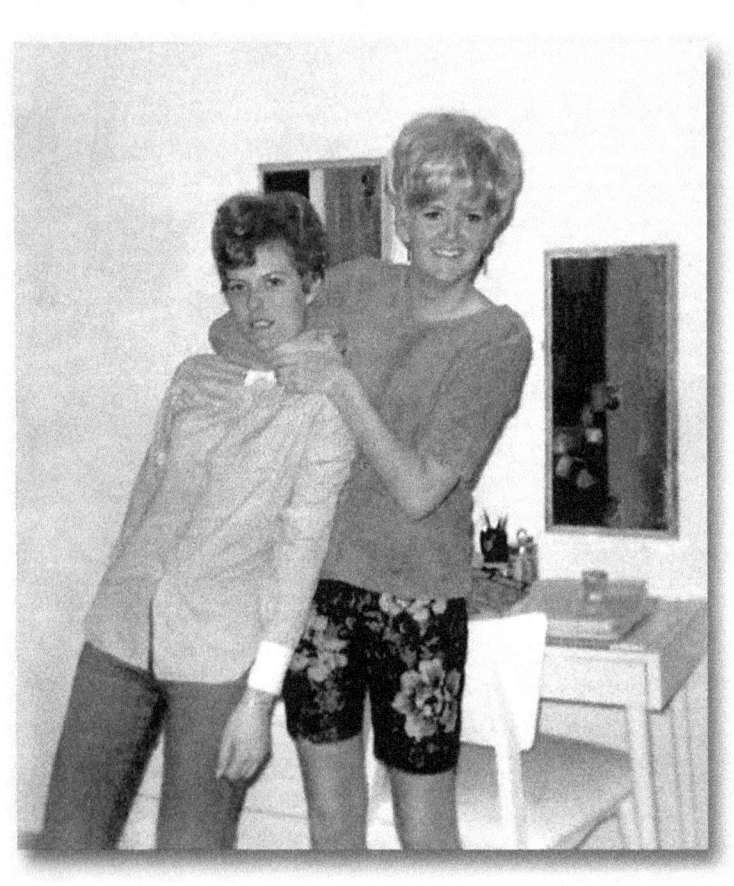

YOU DON'T HAVE TO BE CRAZY
TO BE MY FRIEND, BUT IT SURE HELPS.

The Wilder Side of Me

ONCE BEAUTY COLLEGE BEGINS, I will be held prisoner with only two days off a week, and one of them a Monday. Every Saturday my life will belong to Federico's Beauty School. So this summer, Rita and I make every day count.

All summer we drive around town, or up into the mountains to Camp Nelson. Rita drives us to the ocean, to a little town named Cayucos that sits right on a sandy beach. We eat, drink sodas, and walk on the pier and along the shore.

Other days we go to Springville or Visalia, and ride in her sports car all over the countryside. We take a few more trips to see Murray and spend some great days in *The City*. Sometimes it's just the two of us and other times we are with our friend Dennis. When we have an extra person, we jump into my Volkswagen, or find something else to drive.

Ten months later ...

On December 16th, 1965 Rita drives us in my Volkswagen to San Francisco for my dreaded Cosmetology State Board exam. She has agreed to be my model. This trip is much different than all of the other trips. I'm scared stiff and can't eat or listen to music. We stay with Murray, who wants to stay up late, drink and visit. I'm in a tizzy and scared to the bone. They respect my panic attack and talk quietly into the wee hours.

Unable to sleep, I sit up and say the one thing the instructors at beauty college told us repeatedly: "When in doubt, sanitize." So I sanitize my hands and equipment twice, then flop back down on my sleeping bag. Rita and Murray tell me to get the hair out of my butt and get some sleep.

As I lay there, I reflect back on beauty college. It took me longer than originally expected because I had to take a six-week leave of absence to move to Lakeport and work in the pear sheds as the weights and measures girl. Money was tight and in those six weeks I earned very good money. Besides, I lived rent-free with no expenses at my dad's house. Now it's time to step up to the plate.

As I try to doze off, I relive the routine of beauty school. Each morning I'd put on my one and only white uniform, the one mother washed and ironed every evening. During that time, Rita came over many evenings, but I was usually tired and my feet hurt from standing all day at Federico's. She joined a volley ball team. We were both busy, but we always hung out on Sundays.

Murray and Rita are drinking. They're trying so hard to whisper so I can sleep, but that's almost worse. I can hear them snicker and hold their breath as they try not to laugh too loud.

Though it doesn't come easily, eventually I doze off. My last thoughts are, "I can't believe I will soon have a license to mix chemicals and change the world. This is my big shot at stardom. I have to pass my board and prove something to my father."

Next day, Rita showers, then me. Murray cooks us an egg and toast, and gives me a pep talk. "Relax; you'll ace it, Nana. Remember, the ladies who are going to test you are old battle axes and they can't cut it as beauticians. That is why they're the ones giving the test, not the ones changing the world, like you will. Just use your Nana charm and I'll see you guys this afternoon, Miss Chickie." I walk to the car in a frozen daze and she yells, "We'll celebrate when you get back!"

We walk to my Volkswagen, but I feel as if I'm walking to a death chamber. We get in and look out at Murray waving goodbye. I'm sure Rita makes a face towards her because Murray doubles over laughing. Rita just better act normal during the exam, I think.

Oh Lord, what a day. I am so clean. My uniform is freshly ironed and everything on my body is blinding white; to see me, you'd think I was heading in to perform surgery. There definitely is precision involved. For example, I deliberately choose Rita to be my model because of her short soft wavy hair. I know it will be easy to finger wave or wrap in a faux perm. It's the type of hair that makes any maneuver easy. I think they can't assign me a test today that Rita's hair won't perform perfectly on.

Well, everything that can go wrong does go wrong.

First on the exam is a mock manicure. A manicure? This must be a joke! I hate manicures. They're irrelevant to me because I want to be a beautician and transform hair and make people look better. Oh well.

Though I've never once prepared for this procedure, here I go. Rita sits very still at the table and I place her hand into a small glass bowl of warm soapy water in order to soak her cuticles. She leans her hand slightly to one side and accidentally tips the bowl over. All the soapy water spills over my sterile equipment and towel. While I am wiping off the manicure table, the instructor walks by. She picks up my nippers and begins to nip her own hang nail. She deliberately hands them back to me, then watches. I skip the nipping part of Rita's manicure and the instructor asks me, "Why are you not nipping your model's cuticles?"

"Well, *(Battle Axe,)* you used them and now they are not sterile."

I can't tell if I have just passed a trick test question or insulted the tester. Discussion between the prospective beautician and her model is forbidden, so Rita uses squints and blinks to send a Morse code message of approval.

Next, Rita is told to sit in a hydraulic chair in front of a mirror, and they give me a sealed envelope. I open it and find out what test two is. I have to wrap her hair with perm rods using soap suds instead of perm solution. I proceed carefully and wrap very tight, and when the instructor walks over to check the rods, she points to a large dry spot. I groan inside my head. While applying and saturating with suds, I should have put more fake solution on this one rod. The tester asks, "What would happen if this were a real permanent?"

Later, Rita tells me that my response is a dry recitation of the obvious: "If this were a real permanent, the hair would not curl in this area."

I have already completed the manicure test and am 100% sure I failed. I feel sure I failed this one too. I'm feeling defeated because it's all so easy, a moron could pass.

Test three is to apply daytime makeup. Damn, Rita and those black eyebrows! But she's game for anything so I jump in. I cleanse her slightly pockmarked skin then apply makeup to her face using little round white sponges. Round and round and round I wipe. The foundation is very oily and kind of gooey and seems too dark. It has a dark beige golden hue. I put it on nice and thick and continue to blend it from her face to her neck. I use dark eyebrow pencil and apply the line nicely, following along her arch, then I apply red rouge to her cheeks. Slowly, I turn her around towards the mirror. Rita only looks at her reflection for a split second before one of her extra dark eyebrows travels up her forehead. She looks at me from the reflection in the mirror as I stand rigid behind her. Rita, with her famous dead stare and one raised eyebrow, looks exactly like a well-worn, greasy, middle-aged hooker.

We are not allowed to talk, and I am struggling to hold in my laughter, so I bend over and pretend to lace my shoe. I whisper, "Please stop, Rita. Don't look at yourself or I might wet my pants." As soon as I've gathered myself enough to stand back up behind her chair and wait for the tester, Rita smirks and follows my instruction: she looks away from the mirror and turns her gaze instead in the exact direction of my crotch. I step away from her to keep from laughing out loud. I bite my lip real hard and want to say how sorry I am for what I've done to her face, but I force myself to look away while Rita turns her attention back to her ghastly reflection.

Eventually, mercifully, the exam is over. A woman tells me it takes about two weeks to get the results. Ugh, I groan in my head, two weeks of not knowing. Then the lady adds, "Well, sometimes it takes three weeks." I want to throw up. Suddenly I realize I never got to do finger waves, the one thing I had practiced on Rita with precision. It was the main reason I chose her as my model. That's a big fat bummer.

Back at Murray's, Rita and I talk about the insanity of the State Board. I'm still reeling from all my mistakes and from the tricks the instructors do to trip students up on purpose. Rita and Murray laugh, drink beer and ridicule me to death. I'm deflated so I make a good target. We all nearly die laughing when Rita tells Murray of my quick answers and anal performance. But I have no recollection of any clever answers, just of bombing. When Rita finishes telling about the hooker make up, Murray yells, "Nana, what the hell did you put on her face, spackling?"

Rita speaks up and says, "Nana thought the test read, "Nighttime make-up for a dark-complected streetwalker." We roll on the floor. Rita just smirks, and shakes her head.

As good as Rita is at telling stories, she also likes to listen to them, tossing out sharp-as-knives one liners along the way. Once we finally get control after the last story, Rita asks me to tell Murray about the first haircut I ever gave her.

Ok, this will be a gas to tell you Murray, now listen. Rita asks me to cut bangs for her. No big deal. I've logged over 1,000 hours, and know I can ace this. Hollywood here I come. I pull her curly bangs down in front of her nose and take a few snips across her forehead. Something falls past her eyes. She says, "Nana, what was that? Seriously. Something just fell in front of my face. Was there a bug in my hair? Did you see a big bug?" I'm surprised by this outburst so I glance down and look closely at her lap. There, sitting on the gold plastic cutting drape, lay something curved and black. I had just cut off one of her eyebrows.

Well, if a professional makes a mistake like this, she will fix it somehow. So I move to the back of the chair and stand there, trying to think what to do. I swallow.

Rita finally says, "Well, are you going to stand there all day or tell me what just fell in my lap?" I have no choice but to throw professionalism out the window. I place both hands on the back of the hydraulic chair and scream a deep belly laugh so strong I have to cross my legs and hold on tight. Tears run down my face and Rita just sits there straight-faced, looking at herself. She tries to raise her eyebrow up in her signature way, but it happens to be the one that is on her lap.

Murray is yelling at me that I am an F-ing moron, an idiot, and Rita is chugging her upper body forward, trying not to laugh so I can continue the story. I wipe my face and go on.

Rita sits there, staring at me in the mirror, then very quietly and slowly says, "Nana, get a grip. You're losing control. Stop laughing. You're gonna drool on yourself. And get a Kleenex while you're at it." This makes me laugh even harder. Everyone around us is watching and I have to wipe my eyes with a little white neck towel. I blow my nose, and gasp for air. Whew. I sit down next to Rita and start to regain my composure. Rita looks into the mirror and in very slow direct words she orders, "Now put it back." Of course this makes me howl to the moon, and I rock back and forth with laughter and tears.

We share many more stories about me messing up Rita's hair. Like the time I try to frost her hair using a thin shower cap instead of a frost cap, which is made of super thick rubber so it won't tear. The shower cap springs holes and leaks bleach all over the top of her head instead of staying only on the fine hairs I pull through the cap with a crochet hook. When I take the shower cap off, Rita's hair looks like an eagle just flew over and aimed its golden poop at the top of her head.

She sits at my kitchen table while Mother is cooking us dinner and Rita states, "You do know how to fix this." Then, less certain, "Right, Nana?"

Murray suggests we continue the saga of my abusive relationship with Rita over Chinese food.

Over wontons and egg rolls, Murray asks how the story of the missing eyebrow ends. Well, after I finally manage to get a grip, I pull more of her hair forward from the top of her head and barely trim the ends so her bangs will be long enough to cover her forehead. This little hair trickery hides her missing eyebrow. On our way home, we stop in a men's store and Rita buys a fedora hat and wears it around town so her bangs are unable to fly back and expose her missing eyebrow.

"And what about fixing the eagle-flew-over-my-head look?" Murray asks. I continue the story. We drive to Smiths Market to buy a box of color. Rita is wearing my mother's scarf on her head and looks like a peasant. We drive back to mother's duplex and dump the dye on Rita's head. With a stroke of luck, it matches her original color perfectly and no one would ever know there was a little accident.

Rita and I sip hot tea and read our fortunes. It seems mundane, but it demonstrates what a loyal client Rita is. Despite my early floundering, I do finally get the hang of doing hair, and we are both happy. Murray refuses to let me touch her hair for ten years.

These stories and the joy and freedom they make me feel are not to go on forever. The memories of our many visits to San Francisco—the ones of Rita as my model and Murray as our sounding board—these memories are a gift today. That first summer, and in the many years that follow, our friendship flourishes and the three of us continue to share loud, crazy laughs and wild road trips.

The next time we go up to visit Murray, she tells us she has an important job interview. Dashing out her apartment's double doors, she trips on the stairs and rolls to the bottom. She hops up, dashes back upstairs, wipes the blood off her shins, changes her nylons and runs back down the stairs. Murray doesn't even miss the city bus. She not only gets to the interview on time, she gets the job! She sure put those long legs to good use.

When she walks in for her interview, her usually slicked back hair is frizzing all around her face and not smooth in her signature sophisticated bun. She looks down and notices that her shins are bleeding through her nylons in a few spots. We kid her about this mishap and accuse her of being a total spazomatic.

Our next trip to San Francisco is with Dennis. It's a beautiful day in *The City* with the sun on our backs as we walk down the streets toward the open air Cost Plus arena. We're close to the Wharf, life is good and so is the weather. Rita walks around and looks at the pottery. I stay close to Dennis because he has good taste and lots of funny things to say about every item. Suddenly we hear a faint cry, "Help! Rita, Banana, help!" We walk from two different directions toward the whining voice and find Murray. She's been looking at the multi-size baskets, and has somehow snagged some of the hair from her bun in the weave of a basket; she is unable to get the basket off the side of her head. Dennis is laughing ridiculously hard and is no help. Rita and I work the hairs, trying to get the weave of the basket to untangle from her bun. But the more we touch it, the more entangled it becomes. All the while, Murray is begging, "Get it off! Just cut it!" Dennis and Rita look to me for permission and I shake my head no. Dennis suggests Murray go through the checkout stand and the checker will think it's a new fashion statement. Rita smiles and has to look away and bite her lip. I hear the familiar moan she makes when she stifles a laugh. But her chugging upper body is the real dead giveaway. Murray grimaces from pain then sighs from relief as her hair begins to untwine. We get through the checkout stand, Murray sticks her hair back into a bun, and we venture towards the pier to get a tasty meal with sourdough bread and discuss basket weaving.

Later, we head back to Murray's new hip upstairs apartment. The only problem with it is her bizarre roommate who trusts no one. Murray shows us the roommate's closed bedroom door. There is a single strand of hair scotch taped across her door hinge so she can tell if anyone has dared to look inside. Rita spends at least thirty minutes thinking of ways to drive this crazy roommate crazier. I can see the wheels turning in her head and I recognize that gleam in her eye. To aid her concentration, she lights up a Virginia Slim, but somehow manages to catch the side of her head on fire. Rita jumps up and starts slapping herself on the side of the head. Murray runs in with a towel and starts hitting her. Rita cusses and slaps herself silly until there is only smoke and the stench of hot hair. To cover her burnt spot, Rita plops on a knit hat she sees hanging on the coat rack and lights up another cigarette. I'm not going to admit it, but I think her hair ignited because of all the lacquer I sprayed on her head that morning. I say nothing. The hat, as it turns out, belongs to Murray's paranoid roommate. We hope she likes the smell of singed hair.

This gives us many hours' worth of material to laugh about and reenact many times over. Rita never loses her cool; she just watches and smirks and jerks back and forth trying to hold in a laugh. Sometimes she sighs like it's all over, then begins again to lurch forward and chug.

A FRIEND IS LIKE A GOOD BRA; CLOSE TO YOUR HEART,
HARD TO FIND, AND SUPPORTIVE.

Smoke Rings

RITA'S MAIN GOAL in her younger pre-teen life is to teach all her friends how to inhale. Andrea's father is the Juvenile Officer, which makes Andy's social life very complicated. Andy is extra careful when she goes home after an evening with Rita, especially with her clothes smelling like an ash tray. Blame for the smell of smoke is laid directly on Mombo, if her parents inquire. So far Rita has taught Murray and Andy how to smoke, and probably Marta and Tish too. I bet Betty Jo is an old inhaler from way back.

Andy, Murray and Rita coach 8-10 year-olds how to play soft ball; the coaches and students meet on the field at Barlett Junior High. When practice is over and all the kids are safely off the field and long gone, the coaches run two blocks to Belleview Elementary School. They gather in the middle of the playground in a tight circle and light up. They are so cool, puffing and blowing smoke rings, and no one can see them. I find this story very odd because I went to Belleview school, and anyone can plainly see everything because the cyclone link fence does not make you invisible. The playground is made for safety; it is purposely an open school yard. Belleview school yard is surrounded by three streets, and is visible to anyone who drives by. One side of the school faces St. Anne's Catholic School, and church. The other two sides face lines of homes. The coaches are only concealed in a curtain of smoke and they're high from nicotine.

One by one the gang from Roach Elementary turns sixteen, and one by one they get their driver's licenses. Life is good. It's full of fun, and the pranks continue. Now, with access to cars, our play pen expands.

Murray can legally drive now, and she picks us up every day on Rita's side street. I run down Grand Avenue and wait for our late friend to fly around the corner, then peel out and get us to school in record speed. We never once give her gas money or thank her for driving us across town. We just gripe about her being late. Riding with Murray and Rita is the first time I experience laying rubber, peeling out and spinning brodies. Murray loves to floor the gas pedal and make up for lost time. It is exhilarating and wrong. Our taxi is gray and pink; she drives a '55 Chevy with gray and pink tuck-and-roll upholstery.

A Normal Night

It's about midnight, and Murray's curfew is inching closer. We walk out of the popular and well-established small café called The Pig Pen. Murray is impatient and yells for us to "get in." I hand her a coffee, and she sets it on the dashboard. I jump into the backseat with Rita, and Murray peels out. Her coffee cup flies off the dashboard and lands on her lap. Her hips are up in the air and she is screaming the F-word and other colorful descriptions. She pulls over onto a side street, wipes off her seat and her crotch with an oil rag from under the front seat. Rita convulses with laughter in the backseat, and I run back down to the Pig Pen for napkins.

Family

Rita's Aunt Margaret, retired from the Navy—she had been a WAVE and a sergeant. She and Marie understand each other, but are just different types of people. They know this and respect each other's choices in life. Rita, sensing a small rift from time to time between the sisters, develops a negative opinion of her Aunt Margaret. Rita has a fierce love and respect for her mother, so she tags the name *Mag the Skag* onto her Aunt. I don't recall ever meeting *Mag*. I suppose when she visits I run home or hide in Rita's bedroom. Later in Rita's life *Mag* will resurface and show her true colors, and so will Marie.

My family and most of our friends' families are very different than Rita's household. Rita has a very eccentric cast of characters surrounding her. Meeting and knowing her family makes it easier to understand why she is the way she is and what makes her tick; her life slowly reveals itself. Rita is eccentric like her grandmother, but in different ways. Her love for cars and her inability to manage money are lifelong issues. Rita is lonely despite the fact she has more friends than she can count, and she has people coming in and out of her house all the time. A constant figure in her life is her grandmother. GaGa sometimes can be too much of a good thing. GaGa is a night owl like her daughter and granddaughter.

Rita has her mother's love, but not her mother. Marie is in and out of their home, and seems more concerned with her personal life than with being a hands-on mother. This too will change and unfold as Rita's life takes a drastic turn.

Rita loves to smoke, and she enjoys the piano, but more than that, she loves to drive. She can empty a whole tank of gas in one night, just cruising around town and visiting friends. Rita is also growing up fast, and feeling her body change. She doesn't know how to go about living with these changes. She doesn't seem to have the shadow of a mother to nurture and explain these changes in her life. Marie does take her to see a dermatologist. My mother  didn't explain much to me either, nor did I ever visit a dermatologist. She doesn't tell me about life and growing up, but my sister fills in the blanks and tells me things about hair and eyebrows and skin. I don't remember Marie being emotional about anything. Life is cool with her; just go with it. Her nonchalant swagger says it all.

When you have friends, each one brings something different to the table, something that will complete that missing link in your life. I know where I stand in Rita's long line of close friends. I don't step on toes, since I didn't go to Roach school, and I'm the youngest in the gang. But I do come on very strong with my new friend. She and I have many serious talks about life, love, songs and the future. We discuss skin care, her wild crazy hair, her complexion, and her clothes. She likes to emulate her mother. Her Mozie wears cotton shirts with a collar, capri pants, and tennis shoes that are called Keds. Simple and understated with no frills. Rita loves this look, and has no intention of getting all fluffy. If she is cold, she zips on her nylon wind breaker or pulls on a sweatshirt. Still, she searches for something in life, something that will jump out at her and say, *this is it!*

All teens need to find their way. Lord knows we stumble now and then, make bad choices and bounce back. Rita's safe zone is her inner child, a mischievous child, because these are the happiest memories and times of her life. Rita's dad died at a crucial time in her life; she was just ten years old. And I think a little something in Marie died too. Rita stays young at heart, because venturing into adulthood is a dangerous place. Naturally she singles out easy targets, teasing GaGa, and being with grade school friends and laughing. This is her secure place in life—her lot in life—and nothing else matters.

Rita is held back in 7th grade due to her failure to complete homework and apply herself. She simply doesn't care. This sudden set back places her in the same graduating class as her younger pal Murray, and one year ahead of me. Holding Rita back one year actually seals this deal. Now she has a willing accomplice, and these two friends double the trouble.

Murray is also a confidant to Rita, in the capacity of a counselor. Murray has a way about her; she has a way with words, and she knows a lot of things. All of us enjoy a long talk full of *Murrayisms* about life and life's choices. Andy and Marta and Dennis are all great friends who also listen.

When I am eighteen and I get my cosmetology license, Rita is almost nineteen and a half. She and I become very close during this time in our lives. We are among the last of the close gang of pranksters and Hag Hollow juveniles still in town. We are the last of the *Mohicans*. Most others have married, become parents, or moved away to college, and some never to return. Rita and I get together every day after work, or travel on weekends. She drags me around to bars after work and I'm tired, but she just keeps going until closing time. Lots of times I tell her goodbye and head home.

Mickey and Larry are still in town but not as free as Rita needs, plus they are mature, like the rest of us only try to be. Betty Jo moves south, to Bakersfield. Marta is still in town, working at the bank; she spends her after hours and weekends with her friend Joanne, because Rita likes to go to bars, and Marta doesn't.

The gang begins to thin out as time moves on. We open our minds and hearts to seek adventure, find new territory and search for a mate.

I have no proof, but I'm sure Rita instructs Tish how to smoke— their friendship is as tight as ever. I can't count how many times Rita and Murray help Tish crawl out her bedroom window so she can party with us. Tish has super strict parents and Rita wants to show her the ropes, including the one hanging out her bedroom window.

I'm still refusing to inhale and this has no effect on Rita, who now decides to teach me how to blow smoke rings. She instructs me to take a puff, but reminds me not to let the smoke go into my throat, and just to hold the smoke in my mouth. She tells me, "Use your tongue and your inside cheek muscles, and push out while your mouth gently blows big circles of smoke." I watch her throat and the way she works her muscles and try to copy her.

There we sit, on the trunk of her car, up on Scenic Heights blowing smoke rings high into the sky, and we take a sip of Root Beer now and then. I'm sure she secretly thinks this will be my gateway to the *Land of Inhale,* but it doesn't work because I don't want to learn this technique. I purposely keep the smoke out of my lungs and tell her, "If it's the last thing I have left in my life, it'll be virgin lungs." She chokes on her smoke and coughs.

Marie sometimes house sits for friends who live on Scenic Heights. The house where she stays is huge and it's one of the last houses before the turnabout. Rita visits, and she goes outside to retrieve something from her car. She sees headlights coming up Highland Drive, so she waits, thinking it's friends. She sees who it is; it's a girl we hang out with sometimes, a popular cheerleader from Rita's graduating class, and she's with a local guy. They turn around in the large dirt parking lot and park right in front of the house where Rita is standing. They begin to make out and slide down into the seat. Soon, the car begins to rock back and forth. Rita goes back inside the house and never says a word to Mozie. But from this day forward, she tags a new name to this area, "The Scenic Heights Riding Academy."

Rita is a loyal hair client of mine; I have to give her credit for hanging with me and taking many chances. Once when she is speeding down Hwy 99, she is followed by two women. She drives downtown and stops at a light. They pull up next to her Austin Healey and ask, "Who does your hair?" and add, "It never moves."

Rita sends them to the *Starlite Salon*. My secret weapon is liquid lacquer in a hand-held glass container with a black rubber pump, the same as taking blood pressure. I call it, "Stop a Bird in Flight."

Marta bleaches out her flame orange hair to a platinum blonde, and so does Joanne. I snap a picture of Marta and place an ad in the local newspaper and name her hairdo *The Whipped Cream*.

Rita's début in the local paper is her hair in a bubble with a flip on one side; we call this one *Catch a Wave*. Joanie wears huge barrel curls on the top and back of her head; we name this up do *The GTO*. Life is fun and Rita loves to get her hair cut and styled. She also loves to drive fast in her sports car with the top down. Her *Catch a Wave* never moves. Judy (Burger) has a longer version of a bubble. Her hair is cut to her chin, like Barbara Streisand on the cover of her *People* album. It is smooth with a side bang and I spray the hell out of her hair so she can ride horses and gallop like Annie Oakley and never worry, because her hair doesn't move either. She is one sexy cowgirl.

1965

Many girls want a haircut like the Beatles. There are no blow dryers available for us to use in the mid 60s, so we have to think out of the box. I ask Rita to be my Beatles model and she agrees on three conditions:

1. I have to bring her a drink through the red, diamond-tuck door that leads into the Starlite Bar.

2. We have to do this project on a Sunday and lock the front door.

3. We must wash it out immediately so no one will see.

It works, thanks to Rita *Beatle-head*. I cut the hair like the Beatles, a version of the Vidal Sassoon, cut above the ears with long bangs. Then I open a box of Kotex and put one on the client's forehead and clip it to the sides of her hair, using the little cotton tabs. I carefully comb the long bangs over the top of the pad. The client goes under the dryer with a cocktail. There they sit: a line of four or five women sitting under hooded dryers sipping Vodka Gimlets, or Cosmopolitans, each woman with a white Kotex on her forehead. Classic. My one regret in life as a hairdresser is not snapping a picture of Rita, my guinea pig. Rita sits under the hood of the dryer, sipping a drink with one hand and flipping me the bird with the other, and all the while she has a big white Kotex clipped to her forehead!

Eventually I decide to move, because doing hair all day and then going to bars at night is not what I want out of life. There are slim pickings in our town, so I tell Rita I'm ready to bail. I need to move to a town that has more to offer for a hairdresser and a social life. Rita drives us to Bobbie's house, and we sit on her couch and Bobbie gives us a map of California. The three of us spread it out on her coffee table and begin to search for a new town. Well, I search. Bobbie and Rita smoke.

L.A. is too crowded, the coast too windy, the valley too hot, the Bay Area too foggy. I give up and phone Grandma who tells me she heard Chico has really big trees, and a University, and the weather is the same as Porterville, but greener. Thanks Grandma.

Rita helps fold and pack up my clothes, then I hug my mother and Rita gets a good tight squeeze and we say goodbye. Heading north in my green VW with my license to do hair, I never look back.

1966

Soon after I move into a small house in Chico, the phone rings and it's Rita. She wants to drive up for a weekend with Murray and check out my new digs. She asks for my address and I tell her, "I live on Normal Street." She accuses me of lying, and demands I tell her the truth. "No," I explain. "Seriously Rita, listen, didn't we already have this conversation once before? You accused me of being a liar when I said I lived on Grand Avenue. No really, I live on Normal Street." This conversation is absurd and makes us both laugh. "Yes I do. I live on Normal Street, across from the Yum Yum apartments." She again says I'm a liar and threatens me with bodily harm if I am leading her on a wild goose chase. Three weeks later, on a Friday night, the sound of her amazing engine roars closer and closer, and rumbles up to the curb. Rita and Murray step out of the car as if they own the place.

Saturday late morning we walk two blocks to downtown Chico for an Orange Julius. They love it; we walk around and look into stores, then walk back to Normal Street. Rita takes a picture of the street sign and we jump into my Bug. I drive them to *Upper Park*, *One Mile*, and *Bidwell Park* and then to the *Hooker Oak*, which is the largest oak tree in the United States. We tom boys climb all over the enormous oak branches, sit and swing our legs, sing songs learned on bus trips for swim meets or tennis tournaments. I snap pictures and Murray takes home movies, all of which are lost soon after. They tease me all weekend about the name *Hooker Oak* and the idea of me being a hooker, and how lucrative it must be to sit under the shade of the *Hooker Oak* and solicit customers.

They do have to swallow their pride because they both love Chico. The greenery, all of the trees, rivers, and meadows and even the layout of this town woo them. When I close my eyes and look up in my head, forever I see Rita and Murray up in the *Hooker Oak*, both laying back to rest on wide branches blowing smoke rings.

Two months after Rita and Murray's visit, I meet Gene at a party. He is smart, has a degree, an MGB and a sailboat. He is cute too, and ten years older than me. During the summer of '67 he asks me to move with him when he is transferred. I explain that I cannot live with a man if we are not married, or my dad will kill me.

In the fall of 1967, the day before my twenty-first birthday, I am marrying Gene. Bobbie is my maid of honor and Rita my bridesmaid. Joanie and Murray drive up to Lakeport too. It is a small reception in Dad's backyard in Lakeport. Most of my friends from Lakeport are away at college or already married and live elsewhere. We girls marry young in the 1960s. We don't know how long we'll be fertile I suppose is the reason.

I send Rita a letter and ask her to do me the honor of being my bridesmaid. She replies with a ten page letter about how much she does not want to do this. She writes her reasons why, and she writes how mad she is at me for putting her in this position. By the end of her rambling letter she writes that she'll be there for me, no matter what, and adds, "Just don't pick out a dress that will make me look like a dancer in Las Vegas." I find the perfect dresses and mail them to my sister's house. I tell Rita the colors are gold and moss green. Two weeks before the wedding, my sister Bobbie calls to say she doesn't like the dresses, and she has shipped them back to the wedding store in Sacramento. She assures me we'll get a refund and pick out something else. I have no idea what my bridesmaids are going to wear—or what color—until the day of the wedding. I phone Rita and she doesn't know and she doesn't care. Rita is not happy because she wants to wear her Keds tennis shoes.

Getting ready on the big day is a nightmare with kids and my family walking back and forth, talking and eating, and there is just too much chatter! I have a hairpiece that matches the color of my extremely short hair, and pin it onto a Styrofoam head, then lock it between my knees and design my wedding hairdo.

It is inching closer to wedding time, so I retreat into the front bedroom to slip on my long white dress. There is no way I can zip this tight dress or get the six foot train to snap along the back seam just under my shoulder blades by myself, so I carefully peek through the crack of the door for help. Then I stick my head out the door, and no one is there. The house is empty. Everyone has left for the church, and without the Bride.

How long I stand in the living room thinking, *who does this*, I don't recall. Then I hear a squeak; the back door is opening. Click, click,

click, click, the sound of high heels on the kitchen floor, and in walks Rita. She is wearing a long moss green crepe dress with cap sleeves that she hates, but not as much as she hates her matching moss green high heels with pointed toes. She looks at me and smiles, and says, "*Poo baby*, Nana need a ride."

Together we walk through the dining room, through the kitchen, and down the back steps toward her 1966 green Cougar with a black top. Rita opens the car door and helps get my dress and train inside and soon we have white cloth and a bouquet engulfing us. My bouquet is made from large green and orange leaves and long sprigs of wheat, so we are careful. She backs out of the driveway and says, "You know you don't have to do this, Banana." I answer her, "Well Rita, it's ok. I love Gene. He is a really nice man, and I need to get on with my life." Rita gives me a smirk and drives right past the street that leads to the church. She drives one block further to downtown and turns right instead of left so we can drag Main. I tell her to stay off Forbes Street or someone will see us. We roll down the windows, Rita puts her arm on the car door, and I scoot down in the seat, kick off my white heels and put my white nylon feet on the dashboard. We cruise by the lake, past the piers where we, the Lakeport class of '64 high school kids, used to hang out, swim and party. Eventually Rita drives back to the other end of Lakeport, past the Green Pier and Mo's Pier, and flips a U-turn. She drives us back into town, turns onto Forbes Street, and within a few short blocks she pulls into the parking lot of the church. We don't speak. The sound of gravel from our high heels is the sound I can still hear today.

Rita carries my train and we make it inside. I feel sick. I am so scared I want to pass out. Rita is in a panic too, as she has never worn heels this high, and she is afraid of the three carpeted steps up to the altar.

Bud, Gene's brother, tells her he'll hold her arm, and that she can lean on him. The problem with this is Bud broke his foot a few days before but insists he feels ok. He stands tall next to his brother and waits for Rita.

The music begins and up walks Rita, so slim and beautiful in her long dress with matching moss green netting over her forehead, and a moss green velvet bow. She gets to the carpeted steps and makes it up one step. Bud moves down and reaches out to take her arm, and on the second step Rita stubs her pointed shoe. She falls forward and her unexpected move throws Bud off balance and he has no leverage, and they both fall forward, Bud to his knees and Rita onto one knee in a running position, with her back leg still on the first step. This scene is played out to the pipe organ music of *Somewhere My Love*, from the movie Doctor Zhivago.

Bobbie walks up the aisle in her mustard colored crepe dress, Ricky the ring bearer follows, then Tammy the flower girl, who drops one pedal at a time in slow motion. Then, here comes the bride with my dad. I am too embarrassed to walk down the aisle, so I ordered an extra thick veil. It is so thick my head looks like a big white explosion of net, and my face is semi hidden. Dad holds my elbow with a very tight grip so I won't pass out as he guides me to a better life.

What is crystal clear in my memory about this day is Rita, the only person to rescue me. Rita, who took us for a drive. And Rita, whose large green eyes lock with mine as I step upwards toward the altar into an adult world.

Rita and I continue to see each other often because four months after our wedding Gene is transferred to Bakersfield, which is only 65 miles from our hometown. Rita drives to our house often and stays the night. We cook together and play games. Sometimes on a Saturday she'll drive down with Dennis, Norman, and Marta. Sometimes following in their own car will be Larry and Mickey with Betty Jo. We play Pit or cards and life is good.

No matter how many miles apart, we manage to keep our group tightly woven, our friendships deepen and we continued to mature as our lives unfold and we stumble into place.

TRULY GREAT FRIENDS ARE HARD TO FIND,
DIFFICULT TO LEAVE, AND IMPOSSIBLE TO FORGET.

Canada or Bust

MURRAY AND RITA decide the three of us should take a two week road trip all the way up to Vancouver Island, and camp all the way. First of all, my boss Tony says no, I can't take time off from work. I beg and remind him of all kinds of reasons why I should be able to go. Then, a week later the mail arrives at the Starlite Salon; it is addressed to Tony. The typed letter is a plea for my freedom, for a two week educational journey, but my unavailability to leave work throws us for a loop as freedom is our right. The letter also states how much I need time away and how much I respect my boss, and it reminds him that I'm a good employee. The letter is signed, *The Phantom*. I know it is Murray's handwriting at the bottom of the page. Tony reads it and begins to chuckle, but he keeps it for a few days. He is thinking about what to do and finally tells me that the letter is the funniest letter he's ever read, "Now go vamanos."

I ask my dad if we can borrow his new car, a blue 1965 Mustang, and he says yes! Now we make a list of our needs. Number one on our list is to buy matching jackets. Rita and I find an Army Surplus store in Bakersfield. To our delight, we find matching heavy canvas cotton pullovers. These jackets are waterproof and have hoods, many pockets and are an obnoxious orange. We purchase three.

We save our money for food and gas and tickets for the ferry boat ride from Washington to Vancouver Island; we save money for motels and collect addresses to send postcards and make long distance calls. Murray is already in town and the three of us pile into my VW and drive to my dad's house in Lakeport, a four hour drive. Rita asks him if he has any cardboard she can have.

Dad comes back from his garage with a huge piece. She cuts it to size, about twelve inches by ten inches, and begins to write something on the cardboard. Rita now asks him for some heavy tape, and places this square in the inside back window on his car: Just Married. We jump in with maps, the radio blasting, and wearing our orange matching pullovers. We shove our bulky square suit cases, ice chests, and sleeping bags into the trunk and part of the backseat. We wave goodbye to my Dad and Marion; they are tickled, and wave to us and clap at the sign in the back of the car window.

Murray, our driver, plops on her new hat, or as Rita refers to it, "that damn hat." Her hat is about twenty-four inches across; it's round, navy blue, surrounded with fringe on the edges, and has a cord she secures tightly just under her chin to hold it in place. She drives the Mustang as if nothing is wrong, puffing on a cigarette while Rita and I sit with a blocked view. Later Rita drives for a while and we get to see the redwoods and find a place to stop for lunch at a deli.

Murray drives again and this results in our missing most of the Oregon coastline. Rita and I hear it is a spectacular view, but we have no way of knowing if this is true or not. Oh, we actually do catch glimpses of a wave, a slice of blue water and a cliff now and then, in between her fringe and brim.

Rita blows a cork and yells, "Pull over!"

Murray finds a spot for us to view the shore and tells Rita, "Quit your bitchin'!" Rita goes berserk. It's all a well-rehearsed act; we jump out of the car and hike down a sandy path to the beach.

The beach is an endless stretch of sand dotted with piles of driftwood, white waves move in, and foam sneaks up to the shoreline creating an uneven white line of bubbles. The hillsides and cliffs are covered with green and maroon plants called ice plants. We stand for a long while taking in the air, the sounds and the visual, hoping to never forget this moment.

We find all kinds of driftwood with odd shapes and distorted arches from years of being tossed in the ocean. We decide we are artists and we need some of this driftwood for projects. Rita and Murray sit on a large smooth branch that resembles a bucking bronco, and I snap their picture. Rita looks great in her orange jacket and her sailor hat, which she pulls down on her head like a white cotton bowl. We run around on the beach and snap many random pictures and gather arms full of drift wood for a fire later on in the night.

We find a camp spot along the way, get our firewood out, and set up our  tent. Murray offers us some grub she has prepared, and we gobble it down. They clear off the table and Rita retrieves this green folded tube of flannel from her suitcase. Hello Rita, I should have known. She rolls it out and it's not a table cloth at all; it's a portable craps table, on loan from her mother and Liz. She plops down bags of corn nuts for betting. Murray is dead serious about winning more corn nuts and so is Rita, but I've never played craps. I just roll the dice and try to keep all my corn nuts in a pile so I can eat them later. We open the cold chest and get out Coors and Coca-Cola—Rita pours in the rum.

While we drive, we use my small camera to snap pictures of the confused faces on the people who pass us by. These strangers slow down to get a better look at the three of us, *Just Married*, and whoever's in our passenger seat pops up to snap a picture. Sometimes the drivers in a station wagon full of kids wave and we smile and wave back, and sometimes we put our orange hoodies up and sunglasses on and stare back as if we are robots. We take two rolls of film of travelers; some are shocked, some annoyed, and some laugh. A few travelers give us thumbs up, and to our surprise, we also get flipped off. Anyone who knows Rita knows this is one of her favorite things to do, so they get the bird right back. A bunch of guys in a Chevy yell at us to "Get a room," and we bust a gut laughing, when Rita yells back, "Good idea!" One time, Rita yells, "Five dolla!" and Murray takes off, speeding down the highway.

When we hit Seattle we are again hungry and tired. There are no campsites close by so we have a meeting. We stop at a liquor store and buy Twinkies, Snow Balls, Beef Jerky and sodas. We drive around until we find a Foster Freeze drive-in and order three cheeseburgers. With our stash of junk food and burgers, we park in the parking lot and eat dinner. We gobble down the burgers, drink some Cokes then have dessert.

We're tired and ready to crash, and still can't find a place to camp. Rita spots the perfect place: Bob's Car Wash. Very carefully Murray guides us in, so our tires stay on the tracks, and Dad's Mustang is safely hidden behind a row of long plastic strips. Rita gets out and sticks her head through the strips and looks around the place to make sure it's closed up for the night. We pull our sleeping bags out of the trunk, plop them over us and get situated. Rita and I lie in the back seat and Murray lies across the two front seats. It is not the most comfortable configuration because our long arms and legs are everywhere, but we somehow sleep through the night. We wake at the crack of dawn to the sounds of cars and voices. Murray sits up and reaches for the key, which is in the ignition. She turns on the car, then guns the gas pedal like a bandit, and peels out of the car wash before we are doused with soap and water. She leaves a couple of men standing on the turf in shock.

We drive to Anacortes and buy ferry tickets for the following day. We mess around town, eat seafood and visit a nautical museum. We rent a motel room and take turns taking long hot showers. We order Chinese take-out and watch television. The three of us put our hair in rollers and sit on the couch eating chow mein on tiny TV trays that are on stands. This scene is so funny, I have to capture it. I carefully stand on a chair and look down at my two friends; I snap their picture. Later when I have my film processed, both of my friends were flipping me off. They're so mean.

Very early the next morning we gas up the Mustang and get in line to drive the car onto the ferry. Off we go, across the San Juan Straights.

Murray removes her damn hat and drives us around some parts of the island, and then we find our campsite. Camping is amazing on this island. On our drive, we notice the road is lined with emerald green ferns that seem like a thick tall hedge. The ferns are about four feet tall and glisten from the dew. Everything seems to be imperial green to mint green, and the sky is so blue you can almost reach up and touch it. The water is deep dark blue, with tiny waves everywhere you look, and it looks freezing cold too. The air is nippy, but our orange jackets prove to be perfect for cov-

ering up and blocking out the chill. Rita loses her white cotton sailor hat to Murray, so she flips up her orange hoody.

Rita packs tin foil to wrap around the corn on the cob which we put in our fire pit, and we buy fresh buns and wieners for hot dogs. Rita and Murray fish and Murray bakes this fresh fish smothered in flour that Rita has packed in a plastic bag. She puts the fish in a cast iron skillet over an open fire and lets them fry. Later we have lemon for the fish and hot dripping butter on our corn. We take hikes around the edge to explore all the sea life on the wet rocks along the shoreline. We drive around much of the island and take excursions on side roads. We walk amongst the pines, taking in as much beauty as we can to create a stock pile of memories. It's late summer 1966; we're young, happy and free. I have no idea I am on this camping trip with professionals. My friends have it together. We hike, eat and play craps.

A young boy shows up in camp—we guess he is about 6 years old with bright red curly hair. He is so cute, with freckles across his nose. He leans up against a tree and we talk to him and share some laughs, then he runs off, and later returns. This little freckled face guy becomes comfortable with us and walks into camp and kicks dirt on our fire. Rita and Murray tell him to back off and he takes a stick and flicks dirt at Rita. She jumps up and calls him "a little shit," and chases him out of camp. He sneaks back in close to our camp, but Rita and Murray are after him like two rabid dogs. Then we decide he is a major brat and good riddance. He messes with the wrong campers. We three snipers are on high alert and he stays away.

Murray buys more corn nuts from a small market a few miles away, and we play Craps again, all night, while I snap pictures. We keep a keen eye out for the little boy, who disappears into the night. From this point on, one of us stays back in camp at all times. The next morning we see a truck go by and the little brat is in the backseat looking back at us. Rita flips him off as his family happily drives back to the ferry ramp. The fourth morning we take advantage of the free showers. One by one we take well-needed hot showers and prepare for our last day on the island.

Finally our adventure comes to an end, and we slowly pack up and head back to the ferry. Coming back across the waterways on the ferry is a little bit sad. We spent the best days camping there, and all three of us want to live on the island. We drive into Seattle then south through Portland, and I suggest we phone my Aunt Verna and Uncle Ainslie who live there.

We find a pay phone and Aunt Verna answers. She happily invites us to stop by, and we politely ask if she's sure we wouldn't be a bother. No, we have to, she tells us, and they won't take no for an answer. Rita and Murray make their phone calls home, and we begin to look for my relatives' house. Finally we locate the house; it's a huge gray stone craftsman style house with great wide steps and a porch. Aunt Verna asks if we are hungry and we politely answer, "Well, sure, yes we are." She tells us that she was having company, and they just phoned and cancelled. She has lots of food prepared, and asks us to please stay. We peek into the kitchen and see a huge baked turkey, stuffing, potatoes, biscuits and gravy sitting on the stove. There is more food than I could ever imagine plus sweet potatoes, cakes and a pie. It seems to be centered on a Thanksgiving theme. As odd as this is, in mid-August, it is a stroke of luck; we sit and begin. The long table has a white lace tablecloth and we three worn out travelers begin to devour this homemade luscious mouthwatering meal. Hear, hear! A feast for the weary travelers. My cousin Marilyn, who is close to my age, is not around this day, but her two little sisters are, my cousins Diane and Barbara. They eat with us, smiling and watching us disheveled girls. Hugging and dripping with huge thank yous, we sit down in the car, take deep breaths and smile at our good luck. "What the heck just happened?" Murray comments, "Nana, you have the coolest relatives."

Rita agrees, "Yeah, seriously. What happened to you?" They laugh and we stick out our long skinny arms and wave goodbye. Uncle Ainslie loves our Just Married sign.

Bloated, stuffed and still stunned at our good luck, we get on our way. Aunt Verna has wrapped lots of food for us to take on our travels. We decide to head towards Reno, but first, we have one very important detour to take.

We drive to the Olympia Brewing Company in Tumwater, Oregon and take a tour of the plant. We have our picture taken, the only picture of the three of us together on this trip. We sit on an edge of a fountain that encircles another fountain made out of multi colored blue mosaic. In gold letters it spells, "It's the water." We are unable to purchase any Oly because we're under age, but the tour is worth the drive.

We drive along south and see two hitchhikers; Murray pulls over and picks them up. We notice the guy is cute with brown eyes and straight floppy dark hair, and his girlfriend has long brown straight hair. They tell us they are from Brooklyn and they're hitchhiking across the United States. They sit in the back seat with Rita. We talk and share stories and have a great time; I snap pictures. They giggle a lot and I think maybe they're just super happy to have a ride, but Murray leans over to the glove compartment and whispers, "They're higher than a kite." We stop along the coast line for some sea food because they seem to be starving all the time, and still laughing. When we finish our meal we split the bill five ways. This is the moment when the girl freaks out and says she's lost a contact lens. We five diners crawl around on the restaurant floor, next to our booth, under our table, and scan the red leather seats in the booth; we look under plates and in our food. We crawl around for about twenty minutes of dirty searching when Rita sees the contact. Rita speaks up in a loud voice, "Oh for God's sake, it's stuck to your boyfriend's butt." The other diners clap. She is so happy, and we watch her carefully pick it off his blue jeans butt, then lick the contact, place it on her eyeball, and off we go. They are heading to San Francisco so we drop them off at a good location for hitching a ride, and we turn east.

Reno City Limits hit our eyeballs like a neon light show. We find a motel, and from our room I phone my cousin Jack who is the Pit Boss at a well-known casino, and he says to come over and visit. We park downtown, and although under age, he gets us in and gives us free passes for an insane buffet table. I'm not sure where the drinks come from. We drink too much and are already sleep deprived. I mean, this hits all three of us hard. We are feeling oozy and dizzy. Rita and I go back to our room in a two story motel. In our inebriated state Jack decides to rent two rooms side by side, and makes a crazy plan. Murray and Jack go back to his house to pick up some tools. They return with a tool box and go into the next room. The plan is to unhinge the televisions by taking them off their wall mounts. Jack works on the hardware in one room while Rita and I stand on the other side of the wall in our room waiting for our television to dislocate.

It seems like a farfetched idea, yet so simple. But really, it is a dumb idea. We can hear Murray and Jack trying to undo their metal stand, and Rita and I just stand there, waiting to catch a television. Jack runs back and forth checking the wall mounts. Rita goes back and forth to watch the progress, and Murray runs back and forth, just because. Finally, Jack and Murray give up this harebrained idea when Jack admits they can't undo the hinges and there must be some sort of safety feature. We say goodbye to Cousin Jack, and forget to thank him for dinner. We travelers are not feeling so well. Happy to be alone, and hoping our television won't fall off the wall during the night, we are ready to crash and burn, over and out.

We take hot showers one by one. Murray barfs on her bed and sits up, looks at us, then falls straight backwards and passes out. Rita tip toes across the room wearing her red and white striped sleeveless blouse and she has a small white towel around her hips. I think she is a hula dancer, and I fall back. I seize the moment and rise up again and take a picture of Murray's legs, her feet and the barf running down the sides of the white sheet. Murray lies there like a dead person, and Rita sits in bed like she's at a pow-wow and puts the sheet over her head like a tent. Lo and behold the sun comes up and before you know it, it's morning in Reno. Murray and Rita tell me I have some killer relatives.

The next morning is very difficult. Our television is loose and we decide to pack up and get out of this place before the manager sees the damage in both rooms. Jack has left three vouchers for food, so we pop into a casino and grab breakfast, then continue home.

We stop along the beautiful Truckee River, sit on some rocks and eat the yummy leftovers from Aunt Verna. We drink fresh cold water right out of the river and continue to drive ourselves back to my dad's to return the Mustang. But there is no way we are able to make this long trip in our condition, so we have a meeting. Next move for us is to camp along a creek by a volcano; I think we're near Lassen National Park.

Travel is not so perky for the three of us in matching orange pullovers. It's difficult to drive around curves and look from side to side without getting sick. The next day, feeling better but still tired, we pack up, clean up, repack the car and head southwest to Lake County.

Finally we make it to Lakeport. When we pull in everyone runs towards the Mustang. We don't look so good and I'm sure we smell even worse. We have a huge job ahead of us, gutting our belongings out of the Mustang and repacking everything into the Volkswagen. We have dinner outside on the patio with Dad and Marion, who want to hear every detail about our adventures. It's real hard to talk with any enthusiasm. We focus on Vancouver Island and dinner in Portland, and omit hitch hikers and Reno.

I drive us south, back to central California, then pull over to rest and eat, and then Rita drives. We drive further then pull into a drive-in where we buy fries and Cokes with crushed ice, and then Murray drives. Somehow, some way, we make it back to the valley and back to our hometown.

In the coming fall, just like every fall, dad has his annual group of hunting buddies over to his house. They clean their rifles, wash out their ice chests, hang their sleeping bags and hit them with sticks. They decide on the food they will pack, and check the coming weather predictions. The men have their sleeping bags out, hanging upside down in the sun; they take turns with a broom handle and beat the sleeping bags to get out bugs and dust. Out of Dad's bag tumbles my lost pink slipper with the pink pom-pom I knitted for the trip. Dad stands there stunned. He is dumbfounded; scatching his head, he has no idea where this pink slipper is from. His friends whistle and tease him while he stands and holds the slipper. Then he remembers: my daughter borrowed my sleeping bag this summer when she and her friends went to Canada.

Oh, yeah. Sure, Charlie.

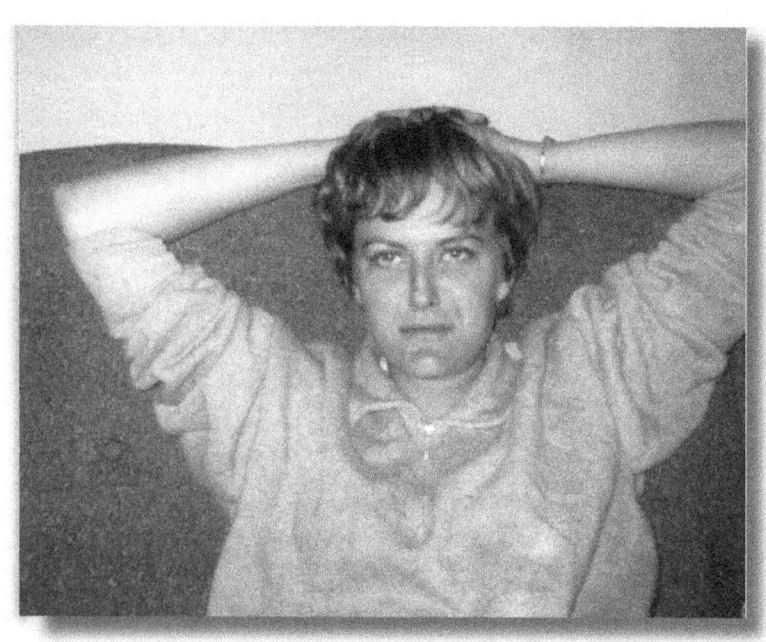

SNOW AND ADOLESCENCE ARE THE ONLY PROBLEMS THAT DISAPPEAR IF YOU IGNORE THEM LONG ENOUGH.

E. Wilson

Rita

I'M INSTANTLY TAKEN WITH RITA. I like her easy going manner combined with the fact that she has no boundaries or rules to live by. Rita wears a natural confidence and this makes me feel safe. No matter how many times she insults someone, they laugh and love her. When I try to emulate her sarcasm I mostly get dirty looks or am slam dunked by one of our mouthy friends.

No one can flash a dirty look better than Rita, and as time goes by, her dirty looks make me laugh even more. I can read her face and it is hilarious. I totally get her acerbic personality, and love it.

I still remember her scent. Even today. A combination of Ivory soap and some flowery scent, lavender maybe, in a clean mix with her mother's cigarette smoke. Rita always smells this way, and she never wears makeup, even when she needs a little cover up for some blemishes. She doesn't care about that girly stuff. Even though her mother takes her to see a dermatologist who tells her not to put anything on her skin, I nag her to use cover up. With her big green eyes and natural black eyelashes, she can easily skimp in the make-up department, her lips bare of lipstick, nothing, and no jewelry either. I suggest, "Just a tad of Vaseline on your lips will help them stay soft." No deal. Her hair is short and wavy and she combs it back and lets it be, exactly like her mother. If you don't like her look, then look the other way. Her hair is dishwater blonde, as they used to describe it. Her aura is one of confidence and a total and complete enjoyment of herself that intrigues me. Life tickles her inner child.

Rita has a stock pile of friends. She cleverly balances her life amongst her groups of friends as artfully as if she is balancing a dozen tea cups with a long stick. One particular group of friends—Joanne, Darlene, Bev and Marlys—is in to fashion, big hair and Go-Go boots. It's all so cool. Rita has known most of these girls all through high school. The Go Go boots and adult look only add to Rita's repartee concerning pole dancers and cage dancers in bars. The five of them decide to take a road trip to Los Angeles. I could be incorrect, but I highly suspect Joanne is the driver. She drives to Knott's Berry Farm, and they also tour Universal Studios. They are dressed to the nines and make a statement. All are having a blast and blowing smoke rings, except Marlys who refuses to smoke.

Rita and her sassy friends have their picture taken. They stand at a bar in an old 1800s saloon. It's a prop, but there they are, all dolled up posing and wishing they really could have a shot of whiskey. Back in our hometown, they get together and have bon fires, roast marshmallows and continue to party. Tish misses the trip to L.A., but joins the girls when they meet up at Bev's house.

They sit around the fire and drink, smoke, and listen to Rita relive their adventures with her twisted take on life. Marlys swears her cigarette is only a prop.

Rita's wide circle of friends still wraps her inner child with peace. She continues to search for her place in life. None of us realize she is lonely and to what degree. Her mother Marie isn't around much. Liz's kids are grown now: Bookie has gone to Viet Nam and returned home safely, Ann is married, and Edward is also married. Edward is insanely successful, and this is his secret: he moves to L.A. and opens a tire store on Mulholland Drive, or some other well-known street, and places a huge sign above his tire store with an even larger arrow pointing to the words "Drive Safe, Get Your Rubbers Here." He can barely keep tires in stock.

Everyone knows this sign and everyone who drives by wants to say, "This is where I got my rubbers." Edward becomes very successful because of his clever, quick-thinking mind, which I'm sure comes from his witty mother Liz.

When Liz and Marie sever their friendship, something just feels negative. We teenagers know instinctively this is not a friendly split. Marie refuses to discuss anything about Liz or any topic that deals with her once deep friendship. No one asks, no one mentions anything that once was.

Then there is Rita's family in Orinda. Her brother Bill is a successful architect and is married to Genia; they have two children, and very busy lives. Rita drives to the Bay Area to visit her family, but still she is in a stall position, and her family nucleus continues to be unreachable.

Gene and I are having problems, and I just got hit broadside with some bad news.

1971

Rita is like no other, and as I write today I vividly recall the day she touches my heart. I am diagnosed as having stage three cervical cancer at the age of twenty two. My son Jeff is a toddler and I have much to live for. The date arrives for the scheduled cone biopsy, and Rita offers to take a day off from work and drive me to the hospital in Bakersfield.

She walks in with me and stands beside me. Together we listen as the lady keeps shoveling paperwork across the counter to me. I'm told to wait over there, and soon someone will come out with a wheelchair. The idea of this scene makes me cringe. I tell Rita the doctor will prep me for a hysterectomy just in case the cancer is deeper than Dr. Mundy suspects. I won't know which way this will go until I come out of it.

Rita opens her purse, pulls out a gift and hands it to me. It is a book by Hallmark titled, *Proverbs to Live By*. This thin hardcover book is full of quotes by famous authors and thinkers, provocative folk sayings and cracking witticisms. I look inside and there in the upper left hand corner she writes:

For Banana
One whose friendship I wouldn't want to be without.
Love, Rita Marie

This act of selfless kindness touches me like no other. I thank her and we both feel uncomfortable getting so serious. She nonchalantly leaves so she doesn't reveal her tender side. Once settled in the pre-operating room, on another floor and alone, I open the book and fill my head with sound advice. Automatically my eyes close now. I concentrate and open the book and think, left side or right? Then, third one down on the left. I open my eyes and read the proverb for a successful surgery and confidence:

> *One cannot tell what passes through the heart of a man by the look on his face.*

I have no idea what this means, not exactly, but I know I am frightened out of my mind with worry. Pretend to look calm. Wait. Is this about Rita, who is obviously worried but doesn't show it? This proverb begins to make sense and I can't wait to read them all and thank Rita again.

They roll me into surgery.

Rita returns to Bakersfield five days later to retrieve me. First she stops by my sister's house to borrow her car. That way, Rita can drive me home in a 1967 station wagon with wood trimmed paneling. This is a much smoother ride than her Austin-Healy, which would surely cause me to rupture. We listen to music all the way back to my sister's house. Donovan sings "Mellow Yellow." *That's right, Slick.*

On the way, we discuss the outcome, which is good. I hurt so much I don't know what they have done to my body.

"Did the doctor proceed with a hysterectomy, or not?" Rita asks.

"No—whew—this was a close call."

She smiles and drives.

"I feel like I just dodged a bullet, Rita."

She responds with, "It's not nice to mess with a banana; they bruise easily." On this day, Rita shows to what degree she is a selfless great friend.

Three years later, in 1974, I give birth to my daughter, and my last son is born in 1976.

The sound of the large engine makes me tired. I lay my head back to rest, and think of how close Rita and I have become and how far back our friendship goes. This triggers a vivid memory, or maybe I'm still full of drugs from my surgery; no matter, still to this day this vivid memory is of the best Thanksgiving ever.

I begin to tell her the story of this memorable Thanksgiving as she drives us back on a long stretch of Hwy 65, a straight shot from Bakersfield to Porterville. She smiles and lights up as I begin.

We are still young girls and have just realized we're neighbors. Rita invites me to her house for Thanksgiving dinner. I accept. I'm fourteen now, and Rita is fifteen. I walk down Grand Avenue toward her house carrying a cherry pie Mother made. With every step I wonder why my mother would let me go traipsing off with another family on Thanksgiving Day.

GaGa sits at the head of the table opposite her daughter Mag the Skag. This seating arrangement puts me between Rita and Marie, across from Bill and his bride Genia. There is no prayer.

Everyone smokes, chats and eats, but I can't take my eyes off Rita's brother Bill. Rita leans from the right, close to me, and whispers, "Eat your turkey, Nana. It's not nice to stare." Then, after I take a few bites, Mombo leans in to my left ear and says, "He is handsome, isn't he Banana?" I don't flinch, just continue to stare and eat and try not to miss my mouth.

Rita leans in towards me again and softly says, "Do you want to borrow my camera?" I continue to stare and swallow mashed potatoes.

Bill is very tall; he has thick black hair and the same intense green eyes as Rita. With my plate heaping with food, a napkin on my lap, I sit, transfixed. The chatter continues and the sounds of silverware and GaGa's fine china cling with every taste of well prepared food, and laughter fills the room. Marie and Rita seem to enjoy keeping an eye on me more than dining and visiting.

Dinner comes to an end and everyone scoots away from the large table. Rita and I clean up the dishes, while her cats play around our legs with their strings attached to a tiny red ball. We talk and laugh, stop and toss the ball, while GaGa plays some classical pieces on the grand piano. Kitchen duty is complete, and we go into the living room. Rita sits down at the piano just like a lady and plays "Morning Theme," by Edvard Grieg.

She ends with another classical piece. I have to laugh because when she finishes, she doesn't hit all of the keys with her palms like she usually does. One tiny deliberate key ends her song. Marie relaxes in her wingback chair; she sits caddy-wompus and watches her family. She wears a happy smirk. Her elbow rests on the arm of the chair, and she continues to smoke slowly while she observes me as I continue to study Bill's face.

Bill's wife is lovely too; she is tall and thin with short wavy brown hair. She's a cross between Audrey Hepburn and Amelia Earhart; very stylish. I swear, I had no idea there were such beautiful classy people in the world. This is one Thanksgiving I never forget.

NOTE: *When I phoned Bill for information regarding this book about his sister, in the course of our conversation I confessed to staring at him during Thanksgiving dinner. His response was a flat denial accompanied with a confession: he has no recall of having this Thanksgiving dinner at Marie's house after he married. A total blank. He was unaware that once, a fourteen year-old girl was transfixed.*

WORDS ARE EASY, LIKE THE WIND:
FAITHFUL FRIENDS ARE HARD TO FIND.

William Shakespeare

The Prankster

RITA IS A VERY BAD GIRL. She and an unknown accomplice visit Betty Jo's apartment in Fresno while she is in school. They totally move all of her furniture and redecorate her apartment. Rita messes up the bedspread to make it look like someone has taken a nap. This scene of an intruder naturally makes Betty Jo panic when she unlocks her front door. Rita just can't help herself, she loves to be a prankster and she doesn't want to grow up. You could say she's afflicted with the *Peter Pan syndrome.*

When we cruise around town after work, we stop by this girl's house that is new in town. Nikkie is helping her father open a shoe store downtown. They rent a building right across the street from the loan company on the corner of Main and Mill Streets where Rita and Joyce work. Rita and Nikkie become friends, but I suspect Nikkie really doesn't know who she is dealing with.

Nikkie is a very good looking girl. Short golden tasseled hair, with an amazing Tennessee accent. Her father gives her lots of money for clothes, hair and naturally shoes, and a shiny new car. She and I don't click. I see her as a spoiled princess, but Rita likes everyone.

Nikkie is going out this evening to meet a guy at a party, so Rita drives us to her house while she's gone. Rita picks up the door mat, gets the key and lets us in. We tip toe down the hall to Nikkie's room. We then proceed, per Rita's instructions, to hang her panties and bras all over the room-on door knobs, dangling on each of the blades of her ceiling fan, hanging on the corners of the mirror. Rita makes a bunny out of some blue silk panties and arranges it on Nikkie's pillow.

We huddle in her closet and wait, giggling like crazy. Rita farts; she then runs out to the front door and puts the key back under the mat leaving me alone in the smelly closet. She returns and we continue to wait. Finally we hear Nikkie's car pulling into the driveway. We listen and hear her unlock the front door and walk down the hall to her bedroom. The light flicks on, and we can see slices of light through the slats of the louvered closet doors. Nikkie's not laughing. There's no sound at all except the sound of her dialing the police. She slams down the receiver and runs for the front door and we hear her tires laying rubber all the way around the corner. We jump out of the closet, run down the hall and out the sliding back door, climb the fence, and run to Rita's Austin-Healy hidden behind some bushes. We hop in and she peels out. We drive to Putman Street and meander our way back into town. We pass a police car with its lights on.

We can't even look at each other. We don't talk. We feel so stupid and we realize that Nikkie will never understand our pranks. She's new in town and she'll think we're perverts. Rita drops me off at home, and she takes off.

The next day, on her way to work, Rita pops in to say good morning to Nikkie. She proceeds to tell Rita about her ex-boyfriend who must be in town. She goes on, "He hung up all my panties and bras on my ceiling fan." Rita tries to act stunned with this crazy story, and considers the consequence of confessing. It takes two days and lots of courage to finally tell Nikkie the truth. The prankster is Rita not Nikkie's ex, and in her confession she graciously leaves my name out.

"It's just a joke, Nikkie, that's all, lighten up." Nikkie doesn't believe her, so Rita describes the bunny undies on her pillow. Nikkie is so angry she turns on her heel, in her red pumps, and leaves the room. When I say leaves the room, I mean she packs up and moves back to Tennessee.

A few months later there is a huge sign on the front of Nikki's dad's building: "Going Out of Business Sale." All shoes are on sale and her father ships the remaining shoes to another store in Bakersfield. I snag a really cute pair of leather shoes that tie around my ankle. I guess you could say Rita shut down their business. Hopefully, his reason for leaving our small town is because he realizes our town cannot support two shoe stores a block apart. Besides, everyone in town shops at Resig's Shoes anyway. This incident brings our breaking and entering and stalking episodes to a screeching halt. Now what will we do for fun? Smash frozen pies on the local bank's drive-through windows? Now that's what I call a deposit.

There are some Saturday nights when we pile into Norman's huge Cadillac and go to the drive-in movies. The price is per person, so Rita, Tish, Murray and I climb into the trunk. Norman drives us up to the window and they pay for four people: Norman, Andy, Dennis and Marta. Every single time I'm stuck in the trunk with Rita she always says she had chili for dinner.

Murray begins to warn her, "Don't even think about it, Rita."

Rita says, "Wow, I have a stomach ache ... I feel bloated," and we freak out. There are four of us in the trunk with a spare tire and a jack. I tell Rita my legs are cramping and she says she has a jack up her ass.

Marta hits the back seat and tells us, "Be quiet! It sounds like we have a trunk full of chickens." Then Rita cuts a bad one and I think Murray will go nuts.

Tish squeaks out an, "Oh no," as I put my butt in Rita's face but she is laughing so hard it makes me powerless to do anything. Finally Norman opens the damn trunk.

It's another Saturday night; we drive to Fresno in my Volkswagen and pick up Dennis, Betty Jo and anyone else who wants to squeeze into the back seat. Rita drives us around. We go into the very scary red light district for the sole purpose of checking out hookers.

One time, Rita shoves one of our friends out the car door and takes off. I think it was Jenny. Anyway, she screams, "Police" for protection.

Rita flips a U-turn, drives back and yells, "Five dolla?" We grab Jenny and pull her back into the car and Rita drives off.

YOU DO NOT REALLY UNDERSTAND SOMETHING
UNLESS YOU CAN EXPLAIN IT TO YOUR GRANDMOTHER.

Ode to GaGa

RITA IS HOME WITH HER GRANDMOTHER, her eccentric GaGa, when not in school. GaGa used to teach the card game of Bridge, and she also taught singing lessons. Her husband had been a piano teacher and a voice coach. GaGa, with her accent, always rolls her Rs when calling "Rrrrrrrri-ta!" She is fastidious about cleaning the house, using proper grammar, and the "proper way" to do things. GaGa comes out of her bedroom each morning ready for a new day. Her bed is made and she has two little dolls that are perched on a chair. She walks out into the hallway wearing a nice silk patterned dress, matching belt, and drop Garnet earrings. Her nylons are rolled up to her knees and on her feet she wears black lace up shoes with a wide two inch heel. Up top, she has a nicely shaped bun, secured with chop sticks sparkling with jewels. Throughout the day GaGa fusses with her hair with her large worn hands, and ends up with a halo of white fuzz that surrounds her face. She is busy all day, and continuously smooths her hair back into place, to no avail.

GaGa's kitchen—well, really it's Marie's kitchen, but it's where we most often interact with GaGa—is always full of cat toys on strings, each string attached to a small red rubber ball on one end, and a lower cabinet handle on the other. The family's cats go crazy trying to attack the out of control bouncy rubber balls each time a cupboard is opened. While walking through, Rita and Mombo often pull or kick a string ball and then continue on their way, leaving a frenzy of playful cats in their wake. A tight rolled up ball of tin foil can always be found for someone in the house to pick up and toss. The Siamese cats are wild.

Dennis frequently stops by their house to play cards with GaGa and Rita. These card games last into the wee hours of the night. Dennis and Rita then bid GaGa a fond adieu and leave. They want to go down town and get French dip sandwiches at the Porter Café. These friends walk through the kitchen, squeak open the back door and yell, "Goodbye," and always GaGa yells back her words of caution: "Be safe and don't stay out too late." They walk outside and have a good roaring laugh because it's already 2:00 A.M.

GaGa is a nosy sort of woman and she thinks she runs the show. One hot summer day I convince Rita to lay out in her backyard with me to work on our tans. I think the baking hot sun will help to heal her skin—clear it up from a mild case of teenage acne and give her some rosy color. We are settling in with baby oil spread all over our arms and legs, and begin to bake, just like two pieces of fried chicken. Soon we hear the back door squeak open; Rita and I lie very still and play dead. In a very loud voice we hear, "Rrrrrrrrri-ta, you and your little friend will get skin cancer if you expose yourselves to the sun." Gad! We think, just go away, and Rita yells back, "It's all ok GaGa, don't worry. Thanks for telling us, now go back inside." GaGa sticks her head out the door two more times delivering information concerning skin cancer, and brings us each a glass of water. She nags us every five minutes about sun damage until we finally get fed up! We fold the quilts and stomp inside. GaGa makes us some snacks and milk, and tells us not to get any oil on the furniture. Then she rams it home one more time, expressing her hopes that the damage to our youthful skin has not been severe.

Rita pretends to be upset with her grandmother most of the time, but they have a close relationship. They play cards together, and Rita plays some of the same pieces as her grandmother on the grand piano. GaGa supports and encourages Rita in her own way.

Like when Rita quits her job at the loan company. She feels she needs more schooling in order to move forward, so with GaGa's blessing she moves to Fresno to attend Heald's Business College. She rents a room from a family who has a couple of kids. Rita enjoys kids because she is one herself. I hope she is good Rita and not naughty Rita there. This family has no idea who they are dealing with. The good thing is she has finally made a move forward to continue her passion, which is furthering her computer skills.

After a short illness GaGa passes away due to cancer. Rita is nineteen and living in Fresno. When I hear the news, I drive back home from Lakeport to visit GaGa's daughter, Rita's mother, Marie. This is a very sad time. We all feel it is the end of a generation and the likes of a Grand Dame. Rita's pranks are at a standstill for a time. She is glad at least to know GaGa's death has nothing to do with her heart; Rita did not scare her grandmother to death.

GaGa lived a long life full of joy, music and laughter. Her greatest pleasure was raising Rita. But in a closer look, life is good, life is different, and life is splintered.

Soon after GaGa's funeral I purchase her mahogany caned rocking chair from Marie, and I still have it. Nothing puts a baby to sleep faster than a creaky old rocker.

WE DO NOT MAKE FRIENDS, WE RECOGNIZE THEM.
G. Henrick.

Dandelions in Overdrive

SOMETIMES ON A WARM SUMMER'S DAY when we were kids with nothing else to do, we would snap the green stem off a dandelion, pucker up, and gently blow the white fluffy top. I recall standing in awe and watching, as the fluff flew across the lawn and slowly floated away in all directions. None of us realized then that one day, our group would also separate.

Time moves forward and so do teenagers. We friends begin to search for the meaning of life and feel the natural instinct to fly the coop and establish our own identities. One by one friends move away to further their education or just for a change of scenery or maybe to put down roots, travel, or stake their claim and change up their gears.

1966

In the fall I pack up and move away from my hometown, settling into a college town. Soon, I meet a guy and fall in love. Murray also meets a guy who is hired by her modeling agency to come in and add more phone power. Murray falls hard and is in love with "the phone guy." She too marries, but she is a wise ol' owl; she and Chuck have a small private wedding in Las Vegas. Murray and *the phone guy* live the good life in *The City*, but one day he is transferred to San Jose. They decide to pass on the growing town of San Jose, and instead move to a hip town close enough to San Jose for a commute. They relocate from San Francisco to the Santa Cruz Hills, to an earthy town called Boulder Creek. Murray is ready for a change since she's been in *The City* and in the modeling industry for ten years. Off she goes with her husband to live married life in the mountains, and not too far from the ocean. She is ready for new scenery, and something "different." Murray's phone man, Chuck, becomes the sound stage engineer for Willie Nelson. By now, the excitement of *the phone guy* has worn out its welcome and Murray is growing tired of *roadies* hanging out in her home. She tells her husband, after ten years of marriage to, *hit the road Jack*. She is now divorced and happy. Murray begins to discover her artistic side and we reap the rewards and receive macramé wall hangings and chokers with beads. She also begins to travel with her sister, Peggy. They both love to shop for American Indian jewelry, and they love the South West area.

Dennis is knee deep in his high school. He teaches Spanish, and escorts his Spanish dance troupe to Puebla Mexico. Year after a year, he takes them to Colorado and also to Los Angles for work training shops. Dennis takes continuing education and becomes a career counselor. The high school where Dennis teaches is a short forty minute commute from our hometown.

Norman is becoming a well-known interior decorator with many clients, some as far away as China. He is very successful in his career. He is married and the father of two; a boy and a girl. Norman is also preparing for a coming out party, and I don't mean new décor.

Andy is married and welcomes a young son, Jay. Then she too follows Murray's lead and tells her husband to *hit the road Jack*. Being the cute button she is, she isn't single long and remarries. Andy becomes a mother two more times; Quincy and Jason join Jay. Andy and John first live in Modesto, then move to Illinois, and later to New Hampshire. Andy is a working mom and always and forever an artist. She perfects her skills with classes and expands her creative style. As a young girl, Andy gives Rita a gift; it is one of her first paintings, that of a young Panda bear. Rita loves this because her nick name for Andy is Panda.

Marta is in the banking industry and she chooses to stay in town. Later in life, she also cares for her aging parents as she works full time and continues to build up her nest egg.

Burger is working full time and she meets and marries a younger handsome cowboy, well, he wears a cowboy hat and looks like a cowboy to me. She also becomes a mother to a son, Casper. Then one day she divorces the young dude and tells him to *hit the road Jack*. This is becoming a trend with us girls—marrying young, then coming to our senses. Andy hangs tight in her second marriage to John.

Betty Jo moves to Bakersfield not long after she graduates from Fresno State, and meets Barbara. Together almost forty years, they finally marry in 2013. In high school Betty Jo is frequently approached by total strangers who innocently ask her if she is Natalie Wood, the famous actress. Betty Jo always, with her movie star smile, politely says,

"No, sorry." Rita would speak up and say, "Oh Natalie, just sign your name and be nice. There's no reason to be bitchy." And we all laugh like backup singers.

Jane and Edward like each other and date. One clear memory of Rita and her explosive prank is when Jane, Edward, Dennis, Rita and I, drive around town and eventually head up to Lewis Hill. Edward says he has to relieve himself so Dennis drives down a dirt road and up a hill until he can find some trees, and parks the car. Edward goes behind a tree, while Jane tries to get out of the backseat and relieve herself too. She struggles to get out of the car and continues to slide back inside because Dennis has parked the car on a steep slant. Rita gets in the backseat behind Jane, and with both feet on her backside, she shoves as hard as she can, and Jane flies out the door. Jane catches her nose on the top of the car door frame and screams. Edward runs back, zipping up his barn door and asks what happened. Jane cups her nose with both hands and no one can understand what she is trying to say. Rita speaks up and announces, "Jane hooked her honker." I thought we'd die laughing, but Jane says something else, and we listen, but once again, no one can understand what she says with her hands covering her nose.

Looking back I feel terrible about Jane's nose, but I don't think Rita ever did. Rita relishes the telling of this story for years about Jane hooking her honker. Nothing fazes Rita. Jane forgives Rita about ten minutes later.

The following month is Jane's eighteenth birthday. On a Saturday, Rita and I take a drive out to the countryside and search. She parks her car next to a wood and wire fence and we stoop over and crawl under the barbed wire. We walk all over the land searching and searching, then we find it. Rita has a bag and she picks up a huge dried out cow pie. We go back to her house and wrap it in tissue paper and put a big red bow on the top.

Later this Saturday night we see Jane, at Coleman's. We park, get out of her Healy with our gift and hand it to Jane. To our surprise she is genuinely touched and says she didn't think we'd remember. We laugh and know in an instant that, oh boy, this is going to be a real bad experience. In front of a few friends and Edward, Jane opens her gift. All we hear are murmurs of "What is that thing? It's huge! Oh, errrr, where did you get this?" And Jane yells, "Oh my God, it's a cow pie."

Rita and I try to make light of it as we walk backwards to the car. Jane tosses it into the garbage can with all the hamburger wrappers; which is really disgusting. Rita and I realize we're not kids anymore but we are bordering on being jerks.

Jane forgives Rita, for hurting her nose and for the cow pie, and they continue to be pals. Jane moves to Fresno in the fall to attend Fresno State. It's during this time, her first semester of college, she meets this truly handsome outdoorsman type guy, Bob. I drive up there one weekend and take Jane out for a root beer float at the local A&W. We park under a white and orange tin awning in my VW bug. We each take huge long sips and Jane says, "I'm pregnant." I spit ice cream and root beer all over my windshield.

Before we can say our ABCs, Jane marries Bob, and one after the other, Jane becomes the mother of four. Jane is a great artist also. It is Jane who designs all of the graphics for our high school yearbook, class of 1963. I'd say she was our first real hippie friend. She is a natural carefree girl with no boundaries, and alternate thinking. Her dark straight hair swings freely on her shoulders, while the rest of us girls have sprayed bubbles, or a curly mess. Exception of course is model Murray and her big bun.

1969

Rita and I continue to see each other often and life is good, and friendships from high school deepen. I did divorce Gene after just four years. I don't tell him to hit the road Jack. I am the one who leaves, with our son Jeff, and move back to Chico to regroup.

No matter how many miles apart, and no matter what is happening in our lives of unfortunate broken marriages, babies, job changes, and college, we manage to keep our group tightly woven. Except for Jane, and who can blame her with all those kids? She doesn't surface for years.

Rita works at City Hall, making money and buying more cars, and trading in others. Her mother retires and moves to a small town in the hills above Eugene Oregon.

Life for Rita looks up, with more pals—her grade school friend Tish and my sister Bobbie. The three discover they are all in the same boat, which happens to be free birds looking for some fun. Bobbie and Rita have always enjoyed each other's company. This new threesome rips up the road. They drive to Armona, a very small town forty minutes due west of Porterville. This town is next to the Naval Air Station in Lemoore. These girls have hit a gold mine. They now have access to meeting new guys at a popular bar with a large dance floor. Rita might slip into the back room and play some Black Jack if she can find a game. They have a great summer of drinks, laughter and meeting guys. The three *Solid Gold Dancers* have lots of stories to tell on Sundays.

They spend many evenings at Bobbie's house too, having a few laughs. Bobbie has long thick sable brown hair, she is tall and thin. She has two children, Tammy and Roger. One time when the kids were still very young, her husband says he's going out to buy some hamburgers for dinner. He doesn't return for five days. Rita tells Bobbie, "Wow, you must have been really hungry when he came home." Bobbie tells him to *hit the road Jack*, and Rita has a field day with this story. Bobbie is six years older than me, and four years older than Rita. Bobbie purchases Gene's powder blue MGB and off she and Rita go, to Armona, to dance. Gene has my sister sign a waiver about the car, which is in excellent condition. Since we are family, if anything goes wrong it's not our responsibility. Sure enough, the transmission blows a cork. I suspect one too many trips to the dance hall.

The reason Marie moves to Oregon is twofold; she decides to retire and about the same time, she and Liz part ways. They untangle their business ventures. Now, with Hag Hollow sold, our hideaway in the shadows of the pines belongs to someone else. Hag Hollow had been their escape from reality, and an added bonus and a great adventure for us teens. I bet the new owners remove the sign. But they should leave it as is, because Hag Hollow has become a landmark for many locals. The sale of the cabin is a sad time for Rita.

She is offered a room to rent from Mickey and Larry. The stage is set and unravels many laughs, with practical jokes floating in the air. But also swirling in Rita's head are her immature, mischievous thoughts and actions. I label her bad judgment calls as "The GaGa Syndrome."

Marie is once again on a bowling team and her life in retirement is peaceful. She lives in a beautiful setting, and loves the coolness—the "perfect weather," as she describes it. Rita is welcome any time. With all of the changes in Marie's life, and the selling of their home and cabin, everything in Rita's life, as she once knew it, changes.

She has no base to land on; there's no going home to flop down on her mother's couch, and there's no piano. Rita needs to take the time to think about her next move in life, like a game of chess. Rita accepts the offer from Mickey and Larry, and this proves to be a stable influence for Rita, or I should say, it could have been a stable environment, but it slowly becomes a nightmare for her gracious friends.

There is one thing that never changes in our gang of friends, and that is our continuous laughter and playfulness, and our long standing joke about the Gommies. When Mickey was a little girl she'd run down the hall to take a bath and her mother would always yell, "Don't forget to wash your gommie." Mickey tells this story to Dennis and soon our group uses this name for everything. We drive to Fresno and go out for a nice lunch. We ask for a large booth and either Rita, Dennis or Norman put our name in as *The Gommies*. In a short time the waitress steps into the lobby full of patrons, and announces, "Gommie, party of eight. Gommie, party of eight." We eight young adult friends snicker as we follow along behind the waitress, walking along like little giggling ducks in a row.

Rita tells her friends who travel out of the country or state to send a postcard to City Hall and address it to the *Gommies*. Soon the postcards begin to roll in and it drives the other workers nuts. During the lunch hour, the conversation is always about the same topic: "Do any of you know the Gommies?" Rita shakes her head "no" in wonderment. The postcards continue to arrive and some postcards mention personal life experiences that directly involve one of the women.

> *Congratulations on your daughter's acceptance to Stanford.*
> *Love, the Gommies.*

Some of the women begin to go through files and paperwork, searching. Rita works in the water department, so she eagerly volunteers to scan the addresses and look for the Gommies; well we know this isn't going to happen. No one ever gets the joke, and the postcards continue to arrive, then Christmas cards, and thank you notes.

Shopping with Dennis in a furniture interior design store, we sit down together on a bed with a fake mink throw. The sales person snaps our picture. My arms are wrapped around his shoulders and we put this black and white photo on a Christmas card. We mail it to all of our friends:

> *Merry Christmas from the Gommies.*

1970, A Trip to the Bay Area

Mickey, Larry, Dennis and Rita drive to San Francisco to visit Murray. The gang goes out for lunch and they walk around the World Market area and check out the many shops dotting along the pier. Rita's friends concoct a prank to play on her, a long overdue prank, and this is how it plays out.

Dennis and Murray lure Rita into stores while Larry and his wife Mickey pop into a stationery store. This store has instant monogrammed stationery. They order a box of pink personalized stationery for Rita. The girl behind the desk asks for the name to be embossed on top of the stationery, and Mickey tells her, "The name is Smagma Gommie." The young woman looks at the spelling and looks up at Mickey to proof read the name. Mickey keeps a straight face, nods and says, "Perfect," then she picks out gold embossed letter head. The young clerk cocks her head to one side in question and states in a very naive tone, "This is a very unusual name. I've never seen anything like it before." Larry steps forward to the counter and says, "She's Norwegian."

An hour later they stop back into the stationery store and pick up Rita's personalized stationery, they have it gift wrapped, and give it to her for her birthday.

Mickey, a year older than Rita, is a natural mother figure, with a distinct voice that carries for miles (just like her mother). She should have been a disc jockey. Her personality is always positive and upbeat. Larry is a soft spoken shy guy, but is very funny too, and he doesn't miss a trick. He smiles a lot, observes, and he sees plenty.

Bear is the name of Mickey and Larry's small dog. Living with a dog instead of cats is a new experience for Rita. As she grows more attached to Bear, we begin to see a softer side to Rita. She calls the dog "Sugar Bear," which is also a song by Elton John. Rita loves to play with and hold Sugar Bear.

Mickey and Larry have a good friend Jenny who is jumpy and she is an obvious easy target to frighten—a sitting duck. Her boyfriend is fighting in Viet Nam and Jenny constantly worries about his safety. She manages to pull out all her eye lashes from stress. She confides to her new friend Rita about her fears of losing him (which is a huge mistake), and she worries because he hasn't written in a week, or sometimes two weeks. She worries and asks Rita if she thinks he's met a beautiful girl while on leave. Rita calmly and softly tells Jenny not to worry, and suggests maybe he's just getting some (her voice rises to a yell), "Viet de Meat!" Jenny screams and runs down the hall.

On a trip to Las Vegas with Mickey, Larry, Dennis and Jenny, Rita takes great pleasure in scaring Jenny and seizes every moment. For example, Rita knows Jenny is deathly afraid of fire. When Jenny decides to take a shower, Rita walks around to the back of the motel, opens the bathroom window and leans in. She lights several matches and tosses them one by one over the curtain and into the shower stall. Everyone can hear Jenny yelling out, "Does anyone smell smoke? I smell smoke. Mickey, do you smell smoke? Will someone please check?"

Rita is always on high alert for a prank. They can be extremely funny and just as annoying, but she provides a ton of laughs on daily basis amongst her friends. She doesn't mess with me or Murray or Marta too much; she knows we'll come out swinging.

Rita once put an engagement announcement in the local paper. The announcement is published the week Jenny's boyfriend returns stateside from the war. The well-written announcement states he is engaged to an architect from Carmel. Jenny reads this and flips out and has a big fight with her fiancée. Rita is ornery and gets great enjoyment from Jenny's reaction.

One day Larry catches Rita, their new roomy, standing in front of the refrigerator drinking milk right out of the carton. Rita puts the almost empty carton back in the fridge just to be ornery. She knows they won't buy milk if they see a carton in the refrigerator. Rita is still a night owl, just like her beloved and departed GaGa. This combination of pranks and her all night comings and goings-and the empty milk cartons in the fridge-plus Rita's teenage attitude take a toll on Mickey and Larry.

Larry decides to write Rita a letter, and here it is:

Our close friendship is rapidly coming to a close.
You need to move out.

But they decide not to give her this letter until they add water to the remaining droplets of milk at the bottom of the carton. They watch as Rita continues to drink out of the carton, so they add more water. Finally they confess to her what they've been doing. She is oblivious to their concerns about her mischievous attitude, and laughs, "Oh, I was wondering why it tasted like water." She thinks about the trick played on her, and thinks it is funny, just as she had with her playful grandma GaGa. What is different this time is her cavalier attitude, which lands her without a roof over her head when Larry hands her the letter.

Once you tell Rita something she is doing wrong, Rita is fine. She listens and has no hard feelings, but she has to be told. Her boundaries in the mischief department are invisible. She was raised with a wide open range to do whatever she pleased, with no consequences. Mickey and Larry are a busy working couple, great friends, but not into raising Rita.

Not long after this happens, Rita is fired for being habitually late for work. She always stays late after work to make up for the lost hours. She doesn't understand work force rules, especially with a city job.

Our lives are falling into place, while Rita's life continues to unravel. No one really understands the magnitude of her situation, because she shrugs it off. We enjoy her as an awesome friend and continue to move forward, while Rita searches for her path.

Rita casually moves, on a temporary basis, with some friends none of us know. She begins to evaluate her life, and her next move. She doesn't appear to be worried. Life is just one day after the other.

The stars in the universe continue to line up against her.

We are still connected and lifelong friends. Each of us gives the other lots of room for freedom, stumbling, and bad choices. No one judges or offers advice unless we ask. Our group gets together when possible, and we continue to learn from past mistakes. We form relationships, and some of us become parents, while others continue their education. We continue to mature, and fuel our friendships by sending cards and letters, hoping to never lose our security blanket of deep interwoven friendships; even as the dandelions continue to blow further and further apart, we cling to adolescent memories.

Everything we know as fun and games is going to change in a way that none of us can imagine. An invisible storm builds momentum, and our idealistic dreams and adolescent friendships will splinter. None of us prepare for the tragedy that looms in the distance.

> TRUE FRIENDSHIP ISN'T ABOUT BEING THERE
> WHEN IT'S CONVENIENT,
> IT'S ABOUT BEING THERE WHEN IT'S NOT.

Late Bloomer

RITA IS TWENTY SIX YEARS OLD NOW, and she doesn't seem to be maturing like the rest of us. You know the gig, advancing from a teenager to an adult. The math is pretty simple. None of us are tearing up the Government or protesting, although I wear a POW bracelet.

ABOUT 1970

All of our friends from our valley town are either married, young parents, teaching, or advancing in their careers. We're not out drinking and being wild crazy chicks like we were in high school. Rita needs to get a grip on adulthood; she's in a major stall position. She is free to take off anytime and visit, she goes places any time she wants, and she still plays practical jokes. Basically she is stuck in her teen adolescent years.

She sells her Cougar and buys a Grand Prix, and without selling this new purchase, which is a gas guzzling tub of a car, she also purchases a red TR6. She continues to play games, cards, volleyball, and she still stops off after work for cocktails. Saving money is not in her vocabulary, and even though her dear friend Marta is knee deep into the banking industry, the concept of saving money in the bank does not compute with Rita.

She is full of pranks and mischief and she is incredibly irresponsible. On top of this, she is of legal age to drink. Maybe we are all jealous of her free fall life style. Maybe she is the smart one out of the bunch. Maybe she is the one who chooses to stay free, because she likes being a free bird.

Rita tells me once, in a moment of trust and friendship, how much she loves Elton John's lyrics from his new hit, *Your Song*. She sings, "Sat on the roof, picked off the moss," and then the song continues on with descriptive words that move her so. She once again recites the lyrics while we are doing nothing, just sitting on a boulder up at the Globe. Looking down on the river, Rita begins to recite these words:

> *So excuse me forgetting, but these things I do*
> *You see, I've forgotten if they're green or they're blue*
> *Anyway the thing is what I really mean*
> *Yours are the sweetest eyes I've ever seen.*

The lyrics move her like no other. She especially likes the line "Yours are the sweetest eyes I've ever seen." Her love for *Your Song* is the key that begins to unlock her emotions. She begins to talk about a guy she met. They are seeing each other. He mentions to her, "Your eyes are beautiful, but I can't tell if they're green or blue. What color are they?"

Well, this is the clincher for Rita. She continues to tell me that he really doesn't care what color her eyes are, he just thinks she is beautiful. With our legs folded as if to play jacks, I look over to see her face and watch her talk; she stares off toward the north. I ask, "Rita, are you in love?" She tells me his name is John or *Big John* as he is known among his friends. She says he is tall, has a large frame, and he works by day, and on some nights and weekends he fills in as a bartender. This is where they met one evening after work. They have been seeing each other for a few months.

She tells me that sometimes they go out, and other times they go up to his apartment and lie on his bed and talk for hours and make out. I point blank ask, "Did you do anything Rita?"

She answers "No, we just kiss and talk and hold each other into the wee hours. And I was surprised how much I like to kiss!" She pauses, then adds, "I don't want to do the deed and not be totally ready." I smile as she speaks with such sweet innocent passion.

I respond, "You're wise to wait." She turns, looking in my direction, and smiles. She takes a drag and puts her head up to blow smokes rings.

Back in Chico, divorced, and mother to Jeff, my three-year-old son, Rita and I continue our long distance friendship. Rita gets fired from her job at City Hall, packs up and moves to Fresno to look for work. She lands her dream job and temporarily stays with friends in Coarse Gold, a small town to the east of Fresno, up in the foothills.

Rita lives with two girls who are a couple; they met in our hometown. I'd met them twice and I like Jeanie, but the other girl, Darryl, makes my skin crawl. She is a manipulator and a user and I know instinctively that Rita will be an easy mark for a person who uses others. I come to this conclusion after only a two minute conversation with Darryl. Rita only connects with and trusts childhood friends; she is not wired for manipulators. Rita never asks anyone for money, she always offers to drive, and she is generous to a fault. This girl Darryl never seems to have any money or wheels. Darryl is a mooch, and I flatly tell Rita to get away from this nerd. "She's not your friend," I say. "She's bad news."

Marta relates that she once visited Rita in Coarse Gold, located between Fresno and the entrance into Yosemite National park on Hwy 41. Marta, who never makes a mistake, instantly has a bad feeling about Darryl. When she walks into the house, she sets her purse on the floor next to the end of the couch. Marta, the banker, never loses anything. Never. While Rita takes her on a tour of the house, an uneasy feeling comes over her. She glances at the backyard then quickly walks back inside. She looks at the end of the couch and her purse is not there. Marta, God love her temper, doesn't mince words for this slimy roommate. She walks up to her and looks straight into Darryl's eyes and demands, "Where did you put my purse?" At first Darryl tries to play dumb, she stutters a little bit, but this tactic has no effect on Marta. She repeats the statement, and asks her if she can hear. Darryl turns and goes into another room and comes back with Marta's purse and a flippant response: "I put it in a safe place." Marta takes her purse and tells Darryl, "It was in a safe place. Keep your hands to yourself." Rita knows when to keep silent.

March 1972

Rita plans a trip to Chico in late March; I'm ecstatic. She says she'll be pulling up to my front door about 2:00 p.m. I happily prepare a huge stew and buy fresh sourdough bread. I slice it, lather it with butter and garlic, and cover it with foil. By three o'clock I begin to worry. I wait as the clock continues to tick. Now it is eight o'clock and I am fuming and worried at the same time. I give Jeff a bath and dress him for bed; later I check on my son and continue to wait. Finally I just flat give up and go to bed myself. A sound wakes me from an angry sleep. It's her unmistakable engine as she roars up to the curb. It is midnight.

Her story is that her friend Darryl asks her if she can tag along. Now, besides a long road trip north, Darryl asks Rita if she will stop at a few stores along the way so she can sell her handmade candles. Rita does stop for her friend at businesses along the way, and they also hit a few bars, and they continue to drive up Hwy 99. Darryl tells Rita to please show me her candles to see if I will buy some and sell them in the salon where I work.

Rita drops Darryl off someplace with friends (I cease to listen), then she drives to my house. The candle story makes me even more irked. I smile and look at Rita straight in the face and say, "Rita dear, you can tell Darryl where she can stick her candles."

Rita jokingly asks, "In her trunk?" We laugh and I reheat the stew. She rolls the candles out of the protective paper to display them. I like what I see, but recoil as a potential buyer. Candles around a three year old are not a good idea. But the truth is I wouldn't buy a candle from Darryl if I was lost in a dark alley. Deep inside I am furious with Rita for her drinking while driving and her lack of respect for my time. I continue to nag her in my mind: I have a small boy, I work, and I'm tired. I'm tired of waiting and I'm tired of your crazy lifestyle. I add water and stir. "You know Rita, you just don't get it, do you. I'm two years younger than you, but I manage to rent a two bedroom duplex, care for my son, and work full time." Now she prepares for the lecture of a lifetime, and it's one she really needs to hear. "We aren't teenagers anymore, Rita." And this is the end of my speech. The next morning we have cereal with Jeff, and I give Rita the gift I've made for her. It is a painstaking, technically tedious art project, an 8 by 10 decoupage with lots of cut-outs from tiny scraps of paper. Return addresses, a paper Tampax cover, the corner of a five dollar bill, and lots of ads that pertain to us and our friends. She loves it. She sits down in her grandmother's rocker and quietly reads every piece of paper in the collage. She turns the block of wood sideways and continues to laugh and read. She studies every tiny torn secret message glued to the wood—ads and notes and Chinese fortunes—while she pushes the rocker back and forth; the only sounds are the creaks from her grandmother's rocker and her amazing laugh.

She gets on the floor and plays with Jeff and his wooden train set. Later we take a long walk to a school yard, and the three of us run like the wind. It's time for some deep interaction so I pull out my new book, *Sun Signs* by Linda Goodman. We look up our astrological signs. Rita is a Pisces and I'm a Libra. We read about our nature and which signs we're compatible with and we analyze our friendship. We check our friends' signs too.

Later in the day we eat more stew and rest. When she prepares to drive back home I decide to bring up my anger issues again. I feel a huge overpowering need to tell her something. Something very specific.

I begin with her lack of respect for other people's time, and I clearly state, "Rita, I'm living up here in Northern California, far away from all of our friends, and if you're coming up to visit I am thrilled—over the moon thrilled. But when you don't show up ... Ugh, Rita! You should have phoned! That's the least you should have done!"

Rita apologizes and says "I'll be fine Banana. I know you're always on time. I didn't mean to worry you." Then she goes on to say, "It's just that Darryl asked to stop along the way and sell candles."

I add, "And drink." I flash a look at Rita and tell her that she needs to ditch that moocher and get as far away from her as she can, as fast as she can. Rita listens. This is our first adult conversation about life with rules.

Then, I tell Rita something that still gives me chills, even today when I think about it. I have no idea where this comes from. Straight forward it begins, "Rita, I'm compelled to tell you something, and I need for you to listen. If you have a car accident, and you are in a coma, no one will know to call me. How will I know to come to you?" I stress, "You have to let me know where you are. You must do this. Someone has to have my phone number."

She looks at me with those amazing green eyes and for once, not joking, she says, "I will Nana-Luchie. I promise."

We walk across the lawn towards her car; Jeff's on my back with his legs around my waist. She sits down in her car, starts up the wonderful deep roaring engine, looks up, smiles and thanks me for the stew. "You cook like your mom, and please tell Essie hello for me. And I love the decoupage, I really do." She repeats how sorry she is for being late, then she flips a U-turn in the middle of the street. With her arm sticking out the window, she waves her hand, looks back and yells, "Later Nana. Bye Jeff."

April 20, 1972

Three weeks later Rita is in a car accident. Her accident happens on a Thursday, a beautiful warm spring morning, with the weekend just around the corner. Rita drives to work, a short commute down the gentle slope of the winding hills into the city of Fresno. She has landed her dream job, and in no time she will move into town. She has worked at her new job in the social skills department for one week. She works with disadvantaged people, helping them with their social skills and preparing them for job training.

A man on his tractor is the sole witness. His account says he notices a car with three young men driving very fast down the road; they drive up behind Rita, quickly pass, then cut in front of her, too close, too soon, and too fast. Their reckless driving, whether it is intentional or accidental, is under investigation. This act of cutting Rita off causes her to swerve or she brakes to avoid a collision. Either way, she loses control and spins off the road. Her car flips many times; Rita is tossed amongst the lava rocks that dot the hillside. She lands in a heap, her car a crumpled mass, and I imagine the wheels still spinning. The men never look back as they speed away. The man on the tractor phones an ambulance.

Jeff's in his bed and I'm close behind. The phone rings. It's Freddy, a guy I dated and went to dances with back in our hometown. I didn't even know he had my phone number, so this is a big surprise. He plunges right into the news: he just heard a rumor that Rita was in a very bad car wreck today. I sort of laugh and dismiss his news and say, "Oh Freddy, you'd think of any reason to call me." I give a hardy laugh, but he doesn't laugh back.

He stops me in mid-sentence, "No, it's serious, I'm not kidding, Judi. Listen to me; I heard there's a caravan of cars driving to Merced Hospital tonight. It's serious," he says again. "You should call Merced Hospital." We say goodbye, hang up, and I sit on the edge of the bed. Just sit and stare. The violent shaking begins immediately. This uncontrollable shaking is foreign to me; I have no control over my body and have never experienced such a reaction. I get up to pull more quilts from the foot of the bed and toss on a sweatshirt; I hop back in under the stack of quilts and continue to shake while curled up tight in the fetal position. Finally, I reach over and turn on the radio, hoping a song will calm my nerves. A new top hit song is announced. It's a solo by Marilyn Mc Coo. She begins to sing in her warm soothing voice, "Oh, Last night I didn't get to sleep at all. The sleeping pill I took was just a waste of time. I couldn't close my eyes 'cause you were on my mind. And last night I didn't get to sleep at all."

At the coming of light, I spring out of bed and call Merced Hospital with the hope of better news. Mombo picks up the phone, and it is so great to hear her voice. I say, "Tell me everything. How is Rita?" Marie sounds very tired and she chokes up. I ask her, "Marie, does Rita have any broken bones?"

She answers back, "Banana, almost every bone in Rita's body is broken: her jaw, collar bone, ribs, her pelvis is crushed, her knees are crushed, legs, ankles, arms, do you want to hear about her internal organs?" And I answer, "Yes." She says, "Her lungs are punctured, her spleen is ruptured, her kidneys and liver are bruised, but worst of all, she's in a coma." My face goes ice cold.

I don't mention the premonition.

Marie asks, "Banana, are you coming down?" I explain that I'll call Jeff's grandparents in Corning to babysit, and I'll be right there tomorrow, or as soon as I possibly can. She tells me Rita's brother Bill and his wife Genia are there waiting with her, and Murray is on standby. Rita's car accident has a huge impact on our tightly woven home town friends—the ones who caravan to Merced Hospital to see her—as well as on her co-workers.

After I hang up, Jeff scurries up on my lap and I push us in GaGa's rocker. We rock and rock, back and forth; it creaks with each motion.

Book Two

TRUE FRIENDSHIP COMES WHEN
SILENCE BETWEEN TWO PEOPLE IS COMFORTABLE.

The Long Pause

NONE OF US ARE PREPARED for this raw interruption of our lives. Up until this point life has been a blast, full of laughs and pranks. Most of us tag youthful nicknames onto each other, and our fantasy future is just out of our reach. I thought I'd lost my innocence at age fifteen, but I didn't know what innocence really meant until the phone call, and the forces of nature that follow.

We thought bad things happened to someone else, like in the newspaper. We are all innocent victims of this crime and the painful recovery that lies ahead for our wounded friend. We are unduly prepared for the outcome that is set before us. Those who are able rush to Merced Hospital. There are many cars full of friends for Rita that continue to drive to Merced. Some friends cry, others are in shock and disbelief.

Only a select few are allowed into ICU. Marie is the door guard, the gate keeper, and she holds the key.

It takes two days to get my son to his grandparents for a day of child care and to clear my books at work. The drive is like a dream, and the walk down the hallway to the elevator goes in slow motion. The doors open to the ICU unit and there stands Marie, waiting. She looks like she hasn't slept for days, and she hasn't. Together we walk down the sterile shiny hallway towards double doors that open to a large room with curtains and beds. This big room is extremely quiet-spooky quiet.

I follow behind Marie as she walks to a bed with someone lying there, someone I don't recognize. It's Rita, lying perfectly still; she looks as if she's taking a nap. My eyes stop and do a visual assessment of the size of her head. Marie did say there was swelling on her brain, but I am not prepared for this, and had no idea that a head can swell to such a size. But still she seems peaceful, except for the sounds of the tracheotomy, breathing machines, and the nurses hovering around her to check her vitals and change bags of fluid that hang on silver stilts.

When I was first in beauty college, I remember shampooing a client and noticing she had a big scar in the middle of her throat. Rita will have the same scar when she wakes up, which I am sure will be any day now, and I feel sorry for her. I'm sorry she will have a scar. I can't take my eyes off her swollen head and face; this frightens me. The swelling makes her skin very taut and shiny.

Rita's multiple broken bones are ignored as she heals. There is no need to cast her legs or feet, nor do they deal with her ribs and internal organs right away. She is in critical condition. She can't feel the pain since she is in a coma, which in some ways is a blessing. Her bones will heal on their own, in time. When she is stronger they'll put her back together. Later the doctors will deal with each part of her body and do the repairs. She does have a puncture wound in each lung, probably from her broken ribs, and this is dealt with quickly.

Days turn into weeks and weeks turn into months, and still she sleeps.

It seems like a long time but in reality it is just weeks when Rita is transferred to Alta Bates Hospital in Berkley. She is still in a coma, and I assume this facility is more suited for long term patients, one where Rita can get advanced care when she wakes up. We expect Rita to open her eyes any day and wink at us, or open her eyes and ask, "What happened?" But the longer she's in a coma, the more we learn about head injuries.

The lucky thing for Rita, if there's one tiny shred of luck in this entire bizarre situation, is this: she feels no pain from all of her injuries. Her jaw is wired, her ribs are wrapped to put them back into place, and her collar bone is situated back into its position. The most painful operation waiting for Rita will be on her knees, which are mush; she must have landed on her knees on the large rocks.

Her brain shut down from the heavy trauma, and she continues to lay still. This is so out of character for our girl. It is a tormenting time for Marie. Bill and Genia stay in Merced for the entire time Rita is there. Their presence gives Marie time to rest and mull over her life, or her life that will unfold.

Alta Bates is closer to San Francisco, and now Murray is able to make many trips to visit her lifelong friend. Mickey, Larry, Dennis and Jim, Dennis' roommate from college, have been traveling in Europe for the last three weeks. When they return to the states, Dennis lands at the Oakland Airport; his sister picks him up and drives him to Berkley, where Alta Bates is located. Rita's car accident, I mean wreck (this was no accident), occurred on April 20. Dennis and his friends return from Europe in mid-July. This time frame clearly shows how long Rita has been in a coma, and continues to be. When I go to Berkley to visit Rita, to my horror, she's now been put in isolation with a Staph infection. The nurses help me suit up from head to toe. Paper dress and mask, rubber gloves, and a cap with elastic around the edges for protection. As I write, I remember this room; it is large, with glass rooms to the sides and a few chairs on the outside of the glass for watching. Marie is seated outside the glass walls watching "The Kid," as she refers to Rita. She used to say, "See ya, kid," and "Ask the kid," and "Where's the kid?" This is a very sweet term of endearment from a mother to her only daughter. It is heartwarming to listen to this nonchalant pattern they constructed over so many years: "Mozie, I'm home." Then, from the back room, "Hi, kid."

I look into this glass room and see Rita, still lying still, like a life size doll, waiting to be lifted up into the loving arms of her owner. My thoughts go from a sleeping doll to reality, then, for a split second it occurs to me that she might not make it, that she could actually die. As I stand at the glass, I see an adult looking at a critically ill adult peering back at me. It is my reflection. Rita looks weak, pasty white and not healthy, but the good news is her head has gone back to its normal size. The next question is, "Why doesn't she wake up?" I wonder why she has to continue being held hostage in her own body, in a coma. Something's wrong.

Marie shares with me that Rita's heart beat is weak, and her brainwaves are not as they should be. There just isn't enough action in her once over active brain. Marie and the doctor ask me to step into the room and talk to Rita, sing to her, do anything; "Let's just try this and see if she will respond to a familiar voice," they say. Hopefully a familiar voice might trigger some brain activity. In my paper outfit I step inside and I think, this is just like old times; I'll entertain and annoy Rita.

I enter the glass room, take a few steps and reach her bedside. I bend down and look closely at her face, then look out towards Marie who is standing so near, but behind a glass wall staring back at me with a look I've never seen before, a look of worry mixed with grief. I hope she'll give me the confidence to talk to Rita, but her face, her solemn stare, only causes me to freeze. Then Mombo moves her hand and shoos me on, as if to say, "Go ahead, do something," a gesture she might have made when she was a librarian. I swallow hard, then at that very second decide to go for it, to suck up my fear and make a huge scene. If this helps Rita wake up, there's nothing to lose.

A song comes to mind, a song she and I used to sing at the top of our lungs while she buzzed us up into the mountains or along roads next to orange groves, our hair blowing crazy forward. It is a silly song, and I'd hoped it would be our little creepy secret, something we did only while going fast in her sports car. But I have to sing it; it is more of a science project than a song. I prepare to just sing, as loud as I can, and I hope my bad singing voice will wake the dead. Ok here goes. It's time to get inside your head, Rita.

I bend down and loudly announce, "Hello Rita Marie! It's me, Banana. You better get ready girl. It's time to sing." At the top of my lungs comes a blasted version of "On the Wings of a Snow White Dove—he sends his pure sweet love, the signs from above," (backup singer, lower voice) "Signs from above. On the Wings of a Dove ...." Over and over I sing the same verse, because I can't remember the next line, I'm so freaked out. The second line is a blank, a total brain fart, so I repeat, "On the wings of a snow white dove ...." And this is all I can remember. Oh forget it. I keep singing. I belt it out again, unaware that every patient in this ward can hear me through the glass. Shouldn't the glass room be soundproof? The doctors and nurses listen. I look up to see if Marie approves and she is all smiles. She also wipes her eyes with a hankie. Marie points toward the monitor; Rita's heart beat is much faster than before, and her brain waves look different too, as much as I can tell about brain activity. The doctor walks in. Marie waves for me to go on, like she would shoo a fly, and the doctor says, "Continue." Again I wail this country tune: "On the wings of a snow white dove he sends his pure sweet love," repeat. Then in alto, "On the wings of a dove." With my mouth next to her ear, "On the wings of a snow white dove he sends his pure sweet love," then very high pitched and out of tune, "The signs from above." I drop to a lower voice, "Signs from above, on the Wings of a Dove, ... Wings of a Dove ...."

Rita is going berserk inside her head. I can plainly see her eyeballs moving back and forth under her lids, and her body squirms a little bit to get away from my voice. I begin to laugh and try to sing at the same time. I get more confidence and belt out an old tune from our days on the school bus going to and from swim meets and tennis matches. Marie grins and wipes her eyes as I continue with: "Roll over, roll over. They all rolled over and one fell out, there were two in the bed and the little one says, roll over, roll over." Rita's heart starts beating faster; I go back to "Wings of a Dove," and belt out a few verses. Finally the doctor walks in and says I can keep singing if I want, but really he is just being polite and professional; he wants to me shut me up. I bend down in my paper outfit, get real close to Rita's ear and tell her, "We're waiting Rita. Mozie is here. It's time to say goodbye to GaGa and come home."

Again, Marie taps on the glass window with her finger and says, in her dry delivery, "Everyone on this floor can hear you, Banana." She flashes her familiar smirk that reminds me so much of Rita. Rita's eyes continue to have REM.

Rita remains in a coma for another seven weeks. One sweet day while Marie sits next to her daughter, continuing to read and wait—it's been four months—in a split second Rita opens her eyes. She takes in the scenery, assesses the situation and looks over to her mother. Rita's large green eyes looking at Marie must be a sight to behold. Rita smiles and says, "Hi, Mozie." Marie relays that Rita has no pain, but is groggy. Marie hits the call button before hugging and holding her daughter, and weeping.

Rita wants to know where she is and why she is there, and she also asks how long she's been there and "What day is this?" The nurses sit her up in the hospital bed, the doctor rushes in to check her eyes while a nurse takes her blood pressure. The doctor runs through a series of questions. Rita needs to rest so they gently lay her back down. Marie is overjoyed. The word relief doesn't come close to describing this day. She phones Bill and his family.

Rita seems to be the same person as before, with no effects from the coma, except for her physical injuries. Marie holds her hand and says, "Hi, kid." Later, when Rita wakes up again, an aide or nurse sits her up in a wheelchair. Marie walks back in and they continue their visit.

Marie says Rita is a little confused, but that she asks straight forward and logical questions. While the nurse or aides come in to feed Rita and check her vitals, Marie steps out for a moment—to make a phone call or go to the ladies room or have a quick smoke. The workers leave the room before Marie gets back, and this leaves Rita unattended, sitting in a wheelchair. Marie walks back in the room after just minutes and sees Rita's head hanging down and her skin is purple. She has either suffered a seizure or she fell asleep and her head dropped down, bending her windpipe, which resulted in oxygen being cut off to her brain. Rita is unconscious, and retreats back into a coma.

Rita does wake up again; I'm not sure how long she is in her second coma—a few days or a week—but her second awakening is very different than the first. Rita has no recollection of having been awake or of the accident, nor does she recognize anyone except her mother.

This incident is the reason Rita suffers with a short term memory. Her memory problem is not necessarily from the head injury caused by her car accident or even from the lengthy coma; it is from being left unattended in a sitting position.

Marie shifts into *Mother Overdrive* and begins to teach Rita everything. Rita does physical therapy for her knees and the goal is to get her out of her wheelchair and to walk with the aid of a walker. She faces knee replacement surgeries on both knees.

Marie takes the bull by the horns and the healing process begins.

Marie dedicates her life to re-teaching "The Kid." Rita must relearn everything. She can speak, but does not know the names of things— plate, spoon, napkin, wall, door, car, sky, shoe, food, trees, cats;

everything we learn as babies and take for granted is a blank slate for Rita. Rita's knowledge of nouns and adjectives does not exist.

Slowly she learns the names of objects. She learns to speak, how to listen and how to fake it. She knows to smile in the presence of strangers who say they are relatives or co-workers. She develops a look across her face of frustration, but most of the time she keeps quiet and plays along. It seems she remembers all of her friends from elementary school, but no one who came along after sixth grade; they are total strangers. I can tell, and Marie agrees, that Rita feels safe around me. She's happy to be near me, but she can't remember how I fit into her life.

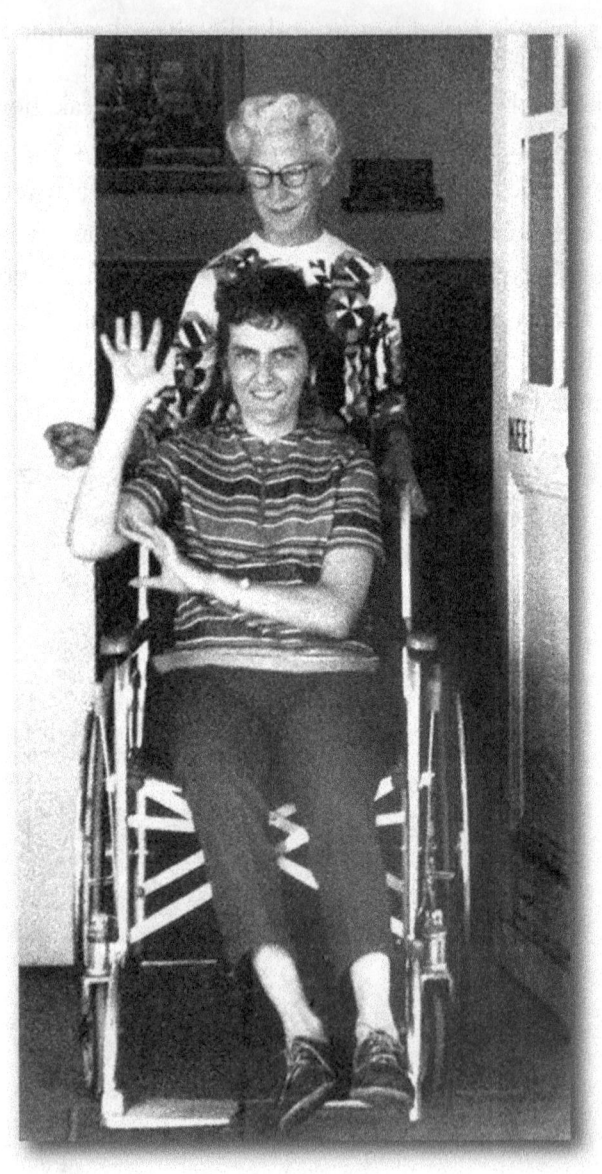

FRIENDSHIP IS A SINGLE SOUL DWELLING IN TWO BODIES.
Aristotle

Onion Breath

DENNIS, MARTA AND MURRAY VISIT RITA, who continues to sleep at Alta Bates Hospital, in Berkley. The mind must know when love and visitors are near. She is unable to speak or respond, but there must be a flicker of warmth and positive feelings somewhere deep inside the mind.

When Marie phones to say that Rita is awake, I drive straight to the facility to see her. I can hardly contain myself, I'm so excited to see her eyes and her smile, if only a smirk. I see Marie, downstairs, waiting next to the front desk. Her eyes are so red and her face so tired that my anticipation of joy to visit Rita diminishes. When we get off the elevator, I see Rita at the end of the hallway, and naturally I step it up. Faster and faster I walk and wave. She is sitting in a wheelchair; Marie is right behind me. Rita returns my smile, and when I walk up closer to her she says, "Hi, Nancy." Still smiling, I drop down on one knee, looking straight into her eyes, and introduce myself. "I'm Banana. My real name is Judi. We're friends." She looks away towards the window, and I wonder what just happened. I hand Rita most of my wedding photos. These pictures are of her as a bridesmaid and us together, with Murray, and photos of our trip to Vancouver Island, camping and sitting on the Oregon beach. She has no interest in looking at strangers or scenery. I leave them on her bedside table and suggest to Marie that she go over them with Rita after I leave. Marie calls three days later to say the photos are lost; it happened when they transferred Rita to another room. So be it, my treasured photos are lost forever. But Rita is awake, and although she thinks I'm Nancy, this is where we stand. I can assure you, I won't be Nancy, but I will be a pest.

During times like this is when friends step up and become true friends, no matter what you get form a friendship. A well balanced friendship is a dance of give and take. I once read that when you have a friend, it's because you get something from this person, they fill a void in your life. But sometimes, for reasons far beyond what we can ever imagine, a friendship becomes give and give. We all know Rita is still in there somewhere, she just can't find her way out. The photos and memories are still in my head, in living color, forever. If she doesn't want them, then neither do I.

Rita slowly learns names of *things* and she knows when to smile using her natural signature smirk inherited from her mother. Her pretense of what is going on around her states volumes because most of the time she doesn't know what is going on, or who visits her in her room. She is clever enough to conceal this.

When Rita is released from Alta Bates Hospital, she's moved to another facility. It is during this time her life takes another turn. After many months of rehab, Rita is released to her Mozie.

Marie moves Rita to Orinda, to stay and recover with Bill and Genia and their two children, Loren and Lisa. A hospital bed is set up in the family room. She still needs much care and constant mental stimulation. I'm not sure how long Marie and Rita stay with Bill—seems like a few weeks. Rita gradually regains enough strength in her legs and crosses over from a wheelchair to a walker, then she rapidly begins to walk with the use of a cane. Her knees seem to be the worst injured part of her body, besides her brain, and her crushed pelvis is an issue too. These are the next parts of her body she needs to repair and cope with. She is facing extensive knee surgery. Her knees and her punctured lungs will give Rita lifelong problems. Her short term memory makes the rest of us bonkers, but doesn't seem to bother her as much as it does us.

Her brother Bill says he remembers my visit to his home with Dennis. He asks over the phone, "You're very tall aren't you, and so is Dennis, correct?" Yes we are, but Dennis and I get busted for having short term memory ourselves. Neither of us can remember this visit to Bill's home. Dennis finally has a smidgen of recall about our visit when I recently ask him point blank, "Do you recall going to visit Rita when she and Marie were staying with Bill?" The only thing either of us remembers about going to Orinda is the wood siding on their home. That's it, the wood siding. On further questioning, Dennis begins to remember the windows and the lawn; his memory triggers my memory of a large shade tree near the driveway. This is the memory of our visit. A clean example of what trauma will do to a memory. We suffer no injuries, except in our hearts.

I think we are both traumatized to witness Rita so crippled and beaten up. Visiting her, and witnessing her injuries, causes both our memories to basically shut down. We slowly regain snippets of memories of our encounter this day in Orinda. Rita keeps eyeballing us, then looks away. She may have known Dennis, but I am still the allusive stranger who won't go away. I ask Rita, "Do you think I'm a stranger?" She answers, "I don't know." So I tweak her and reply, "Because I'm stranger than you think." She smiles at this and lets air out of her lungs as she always did, and chugs forward-her classic way of laughing. She gets the joke, and this a very good sign. She looks at us, then looks away again, trying to process. Rita feels comfortable when she is next to me. She listens to my voice, but there is no recall.

Dennis remembers her body to this day. His recollection comes back and so does mine. But not a total recall. He remembers she was very flexible. He recalls that she put her foot on the couch then crossed her leg, and put her head on her knee to rest. He describes her as sitting there, folded up on the couch looking like a little bird.

I babble about nothing, and continue to be myself. Dennis and I laugh and if Murray is with us—*(Was she with us? None of us can remember)*—we laugh together. Rita knows something is familiar, but she's not sure what.

The mind is as foreign to us as the makings of coleslaw; we are young and clueless. We have no recall of driving to Bill's house and only slivers of recall once inside of his home. But we remember Rita, clearly, and Dennis recalls much more than I.

I clearly recall with accurate detail my visit to Merced Hospital, then to Alta Bates hospital, then to the facility for long term patients. But when she is released and her healing begins, my memories of visits are sparse.

Marie feels it's time to move Rita back to Porterville, and they move in with guess who: Mag the Skag, of all people. Now this odd relationship comes full circle. Rita is happy to see her Aunt Margaret, because she has no memory of anything negative, and Margaret is very pleased to help. Being back in Porterville gives Marie a chance to show Rita their life before the accident and it aids her memory to return and live in her hometown.

Rita's almost fatal accident changes the course of the sisters' history, their little disputes, and their strong opinions of one another; all of their differences dissipate into thin air.

Marie is in the kitchen preparing dinner one evening and Rita walks in. Marie watches her out of the corner of her eye. Rita is hungry. She looks at an onion, reaches for it, picks it up, puts it to her mouth, takes a big bite and continues to chew the raw onion. Marie carefully takes the onion from her and explains to her daughter *the law of onions.*

There are ways to caramelize onions, which brings out the sweetness; cooking onions for hamburgers or a casserole can add flavor. They're good in all types of salads. Onions enhance food, but can also scare off vampires when eaten raw. Rita smiles at her mother's dry humor. End of lecture, Mozie hands Rita an apple. The taste of a raw onion was probably enough to teach her the difference, but she doesn't seem to notice and Marie knows she has a very long way to go. And killer breath.

Rita continues to improve, but very slowly. Marie dedicates her life to her daughter. She reads to her. She takes her on trips to visit friends and to revisit National parks. Then, one afternoon Marie drives Rita to the next town north of Porterville. She takes Rita to Strathmore to visit the red brick house where they lived until Rita was in her preteens. They stop, get out, and look at the red brick house, the barn, the arena and the overall location. Rita seems pleased, but whether or not she understands the dynamics of this home and the property is in question. The next day Marie drives Rita to Roach Avenue School. She pulls over next to the curb and the two of them sit in the car and watch the children on the playground as they screech and run and twirl on the merry-go-round. Marie looks at Rita's face and sees pure joy. As they continue to watch the children play and chase around the school yard, they are both full of joy.

They drive down Roach Avenue past Liz's home where she and Rita had spent so much time. No mention of Liz, they drive a few blocks to the one and only park in town. They get out of the car, sit under groves of palms and look at the duck pond; Marie pulls out a bag of bread crumbs and Rita tosses them to the ducks. Rita enjoys these small snippets of exposure to her other life. Back in the car she drives past the public swimming pool located just up the park on the hillside.

Time for another outing. Marie drives Rita to Grand Avenue, they cruise past her once beloved home where they'd lived with GaGa. Marie pulls onto the side street by the opening in the fence that exposes the kitchen door—the door used by all who visited. Rita stares at the house with a sad look on her face but says nothing. Marie points out my home just four houses down the street, but Rita has no recall. She drives to Andy's home, which is just down a few streets off Grand Avenue onto Village Lane. Then Marie drives her across town to Murray's home. Rita looks, smiles and stares at the houses, but her Mozie still isn't sure how much Rita is soaking up with these drive-bys.

Marie is very clever, teaching Rita through books, memory, visual and sensory stimulation.

One day her friends in town plan a reunion in her honor, a simple get together with friends. Everyone who has ever been close to Rita is there, and they anxiously wait. The old gang talks about old times as they laugh and wait. Then Marie drives up to the curb with Rita. This is a very big deal, and a chance for her to visit and perhaps jar her memory. Rita is still weak; she steps out of the car with the use of her cane and begins to walk to the front door. She is tired—tired of all the questions and tired of not knowing what everyone assumes she should know. Sadly, she doesn't remember most of these friends. There are too many people, and it's too much stimulation. Does she enjoy the laughter? Maybe, but she is clearly disturbed by all of the conversations. Dennis keeps a keen eye out for two more friends, and he closely watches his longtime friend and reads her expressions.

Beverly and Joanne finally pull up to the curb, Dennis looks out the window and says to Rita, "Oh look Rita, it's Box Car Bertha." Rita looks out the window and back to the room, with no expression. Everyone howls at Dennis's comment. The once great friends walk inside the house and dramatic Beverly stretches her arms out to the sides and yells, "Rita!"

Rita continues to sit there with no expression, then looks up at Beverly and in a flat monotone voice replies, "Hello, Bertha." The room goes wild with a roar of laughter. Rita smirks.

Joyce, Joanne and Marta decide to take Rita to the County Fair and they go with Marie's blessing. Burger says they walk up to a group of people and Rita sees Burger, who is short in stature and has a muscular build and sandy blond hair. Burger doesn't see Rita as she works on the booth she's affiliated with. Burger bends over to get something out of a box. No one knows why, but Rita smacks her on the butt with her cane. Burger yelps, "Ouch, damn you Rita!" and Rita, for the first time, laughs out loud.

We know she is in there someplace, but none of us want to be smacked with her cane to solidify the friendship, nor do we want her to begin to use this tactic as a joke.

1973

It has been one year since the accident; Marie decides to take Rita on a long road trip across the United States to recall faces and places. Marie is hell bent on Rita regaining as much of her memory as possible. She drives Rita to Vermont to visit the old homestead where GaGa lived and raised her daughters and son. They camp all the way and this helps Rita understand her life and gain total trust of her mother's choices in activity. They stop to visit Andy who lives in Illinois. Andy says they only stay a few hours, but Rita instantly knows Andy. There is no display of memory disorder at all. She calmly talks to Andy about small things, and says words she needs to say. Andy is a little surprised when she notices her speech is somewhat slurred, but still very easy to understand. It was a great visit with old friends.

In Vermont Rita sees the beautiful trees and fall colors. She seems to enjoy this very much; she loves the sound of the wind that rustles through the leaves. She does not however remember or understand the importance of GaGa's home.

The two travelers drive back through Yellowstone, take in the majestic views, and enjoy the smells and visuals that surround them. Rita loves Yellowstone, and seems to remember her trip there, so long ago with her mom and Andy. She enjoys the scenery; she stands with her cane and stares at the vast meadows and the amazing mountains. Rita takes deep breaths of mountain air. Something in her is coming alive; her senses to smells and visual pleasure are real, and this helps her memory.

I doubt if they camped too many times with Rita not totally healthy yet. Marie probably springs for a room at the lodge. Eventually she drives Rita towards Northern California to my dad's house. Rita loves my dad, so let's see if she remembers him, and if so, then maybe she'll figure out who this Banana girl is—the one who keeps hanging around.

Marie gives me a heads up that she and Rita are driving to Lakeport this coming Saturday. Jeff is four years old, I pack him up and off we go. We wait with high anticipation, and finally we hear a car pull into the back parking lot. Two car doors close, then it takes a very long time before they walk inside. Dad opens the screen door and holds it open for his guests. I think to myself, Rita, please remember my wedding day and this house, and me.

In they walk, through the kitchen and into the dining room. Rita looks at my dad, grins and gives him a friendly, "Hello Charlie." Dad responds with, "Hello Rita. It's great to see you," and he returns the hug, only his is a huge bear hug. Marion, my step mother, politely reintroduces herself to Rita. Then she and Marie shake hands. Rita looks around and she seems to remember this elegant room and all the gold décor. I can tell by the look across her face, she's been here and she knows it. Then she looks over towards me and smiles, as if we've never met. Jeff steps up and she smiles down at him and says, "You must be Jeff," and he answers, "I am." She shakes his hand and seems very happy to see him again—whether or not she actually remembers him—she seems to have a pleasant rapport with him for some reason. This is beginning to strike me as funny, so I smile and decide, right then and there, to smother her with kindness.

Marie and Marion have cocktails at the dining room table. They each enjoy a good smoke and seem to be on the same vein of thought. They soon bolt outside to the back patio. I sit next to Rita on Marion's long gold floral couch that could easily sit six people, but I squeeze in and sit right next to her. It appears we are sitting on a bus. I continue to smother her, and she seems to like it. She is all smiles and makes a few off the wall comments. Her legs are crossed, just like Dennis says; she sits like a bird, a happy bird. Dad takes a picture of us sitting together, and I am so happy to have this photo.

Rita still struggles from short term memory loss, but her wit and wicked sense of humor are not damaged. I can feel her presence. We snuggle up a bit on the couch and she has that ol' smirk on her face. I nestle up to her and it is a wonderful entanglement: me and the little bird.

Rita's eyes have always been her telling point. Her once clever eyes and expression no longer exist. If you look right at her you can tell, because now the look in her eyes is vague. This is very disturbing to comprehend, and it's very hard to imagine our once clever girlfriend locked in there someplace.

Mozie puts her heart and soul into retraining her daughter. This is her lot in life and she is a mother on a mission and a teacher all rolled into one. Mozie will rise up and teach her daughter with great care the second time around.

During this time, Marie purchases a house in Eugene Oregon, a cozy home on a shady corner lot. The street is named Camelot. It is a small house: three bedrooms and one bathroom, a small living room, a fireplace and a small galley kitchen with a window that faces a shady backyard. Rita loves it so much; she loves the trees, the shade, the greenery and the security of her own bedroom. Rita hangs up the decoupage I made for her weeks before her wreck. Beside it she hangs the *Panda Bear*, the painting Andy had painted especially for her.

Next on their agenda is a visit to the Green Hills humane society, where they pick out two cats. Marie lets Rita name her cats, and now Rita has responsibility and something to do with her spare time.

Marie teaches Rita the names of all objects, then she teaches her how to drive. Rita passes the test, and Marie purchases her a small white pick-up truck. She is soaking up knowledge quickly. Rita is also involved with a clinic to help her cope with her injuries, and learn the art of living with memory loss.

1977

Murray and I decide to take a road trip to Eugene to spend the weekend with Rita and Mombo. Murray drives from San Francisco to my front door in Chico. I have two young children and a baby. We pack up their clothes, Dana's doll, baby blankets, and some snacks for a two year old. I hold my baby boy and nurse him when needed. Off we go in my Bronco. Jeff, the oldest, spends the weekend with his grandparents.

I check the back seat and see my daughter, Dana, whom we lovingly nick named Lollie when she began to crawl and say *la la la la la*. She is playing with a coloring book and she has her blanket and a stuffed clown head, and a doll in a pink dress. My baby son Spencer is just seven months old and giggles, nurses and sleeps.

The trip goes quickly; and the kids are quiet; and no problems. Murray stops in Ashland and finds a shady park so we can stretch and grab some food. Murray plays with Dana while I rock my body back and forth and talk to my son.

We arrive at Rita's with the kids in tow, and Rita loves this. Marie stays quiet and busies herself. Murray, Rita and I take Dana outside to the front yard and play chase. I hold my son and watch. Then, shock of all shocks, Marie comes out and asks to hold my baby. Murray and I chase my daughter around the yard. She squeals and runs around the only tree. Rita stands with her cane and smiles.

Murray and I agree we should take Rita to dinner and a movie to try and help her remember us as a group, and the good times, and to see if the chemistry between the three of us is as powerful as ever. Marie encourages us to go out, to take Rita out. "You girls need to go out and have some fun." But the kids, well, Marie says she'll watch the kids and I know instantly I'll be worried sick. But I feed them, bathe Dana and dress them for bed. Marie has borrowed a crib and everything is in place in the front bedroom, except for my confidence in Marie's nurturing skills.

I go over and over the dangers of quilts: "It's colder up here than in Chico. They have warm fleece zip ups, but I don't want the door shut because their faces will get cold and their hands too. I don't want you to tuck in the quilts tight around their necks because they might smother. Just put the quilts over them lightly, but don't tuck the quilts into their sides. They need to be able to move and they need to breathe, but they also need to keep warm and not smother," I repeat. Marie stands at the bedroom door and leans on the door jam and listens with that classic smirk on her face, which causes great concern. Finally we three old friends say goodbye and leave for dinner.

Rita talks the entire time; Murray and Rita have long conversations. I nod my head and add my two cents. Rita asks many questions about her life, her memory and food. She's just found an *all you can eat* diner that's open twenty-four hours a day. She has already put on about thirty pounds. Murray cautions her to not get too heavy because of the pressure this will cause on her knees. We explain to her about her knees and her weight, and Rita goes on to tell us about the beef stroganoff, gravy and biscuits. Finally we head home, back to Marie's Daycare Center. Murray tells Rita, "Let's take Nana home; she's worried about her babies."

Rita unlocks the front door and the door won't budge. Murray pushes on the front door and says "There's something blocking the door." She reaches in with her thin arm and says, "I can feel something, and it's blocking our entry." I have a massive mother attack and push the door open with my right shoulder, and there in front of the door is Marie's wing back chair. Marie has purposely placed the chair smack dab in front of the door. Murray sees a note attached to the back of the chair with a diaper pin. This is bad, very bad. Murray reads it and laughs so loud that she is cackling. She yells, "This is righteous! Mombo got you this time, Nana!" I grab the piece of paper with torn edges and read aloud, "Lollie didn't smother and neither did her brother."

I quickly tip toe down the hall and peek in to check on my babies; both are sound asleep under loosely draped baby quilts. Marie stays in bed and I'm sure she listens and smiles because Murray laughs her head off for a while. Rita snickers but Murray is hysterical, busting a gut laughing and squeaking out words like *Classic—Too damn funny—* and *Too cool.* Then she tells me, "You have to keep this note, Nana."

Next morning, I bring my son into bed with Dana and me, and nurse him while my daughter snuggles in close. I can hear laughing out in the kitchen and it's Murray, reliving the note. Finally, with a baby in one arm and a toddler holding my hand, we mosey out to the living room. Murray pours milk over Cheerios for Dana, and makes toast with some of Margaret's famous jam on top. Rita sits there drinking coffee, talking to her cats, and Marie, well, she is in the kitchen and she keeps her back to me and asks, "Eggs, Banana?" She turns around, smiles and we share a good laugh together.

Marie enrolls Rita into private physical therapy sessions, and she also checks all of the avenues to deal with head injuries. Rita hates her first visit to a head injuries group. She complains to Mozie, "I'm smarter than this. I don't need to be in there, and I only need to be in there to help others." This is a two-sided sword, but Marie works with Rita, calms her down, and they begin to visit and see to what degree Rita can be of help to the others who are less fortunate.

This phase of Rita's life in her new home with her constant companion and teacher, Mozie and her two cats proves to be a positive one. Marie is relentless, working on Rita's short term memory and everything else, from hygiene to cooking to pulling weeds, driving and gathering kindling.

Marie mows the front and back lawn, she shops and cooks and continues to do her own thing, which is to provide Rita with a roof over her head and meals, and to supervise her ongoing learning skills. They are both very happy, but I feel Rita needs more structure in her life.

She is developing bad habits and a lazy lifestyle, and she needs more stimulation and group activities. Rita enjoys a drive around the outskirts of town. Daily she stops at the Humane Society and pets the animals, she gathers kindling, and then drives to the *all you can eat* buffet. Marie has joined a bowling league and life is very smooth.

Marie hires Susan, Andy's sister, to help Rita with her finances and to prepare Rita in case anything were to happen to her—*Marie*. Susan is very nice to Rita, but very business-like. She efficiently and correctly keeps track of Rita's money, taxes, and disability checks, and she keeps a balanced bank account. Rita's medical bills are in order, as well as all information concerning free seminars and clinics that are now available to Rita.

Something unforeseen is brewing, and Marie never says one word.

Life seems unusually blissful and bright. Rita has motivation and a wonderful hobby, which is picking up and organizing kindling. She is gaining weight from her nightly *eat-a-thons* and she enjoys going to the head trauma clinics. Rita's slurred speech has improved and is not as obvious as it was in the '70s.

There seems to be light in her eyes, more understanding, and a clearer expression. What Rita doesn't have is her long term memory. This escalates and the nightly phone calls begin.

Only a select few are enlightened with Rita's nightly phone calls. On her waiting list for her new hot topics are: Murray, Banana, Marta, Dennis, Burger, Andy and Bill. Rita continues to phone each of us and her timing is still off, *way off*. She forgets that some people actually sleep. After a few years, she narrows her nightly *dial-a-friend* to just four of us, then she drops Dennis and Marta when she decides to zero in on the real question, her very personal question. Murray and I will be the ones to shed light on the subject. Rita continues to wake up her other friends from a deep sleep, mind you, but she never asks them the one pressing personal question. Oh no, it's only the two of us who are dumb enough to pick up the phone night after night; then weeks turn into years—and I stress—*thirty years.*

Actually, it was often enjoyable chatting with her about life. To this day her voice is still in my head, clear and ever present.

> IT'S THE FRIENDS YOU CAN CALL UP
> AT 4:00 A.M. THAT MATTER.
>
> *Marlene Dietrich*

Midnight Caller

THE PHONE CALLS IN THE MIDDLE OF THE NIGHT BEGIN, I'd have to guess, in 1978, six years after her accident. The phone rings next to my bed; it is 2:15 A.M. I answer in a whisper as to not wake up my husband. On the other end is Rita. "Hi, Banana, I hope I'm not calling too late."

I lie and say, "No, no Rita. Is something wrong?"

She goes on to say she's sorry for calling and that she has been out eating, and she wants to ask me something: "I was wondering if you know whether or not I'm a virgin."

I quietly slip out of bed, run down the hall to the living room, and begin to tell her, "Well, Rita, I've known you since we were thirteen years old. You and I have spent many nights together and I can honestly say I'm very sure you are a virgin."

She is very—no extremely—disappointed and replies, "Really?"

I have to say again, "Yes, you're a virgin." We move on to other subjects but I have to stop and remind her that I have three small children. "I can't talk on the phone in the middle of the night Rita, I just can't."

"Ok, sorry, bye," she says.

Two days later at 3:30 A.M. the phone rings. She asks the exact word-for-word question: "Hi, Banana, I hope I'm not calling too late, but I was just wondering if you know whether or not I'm a virgin."

I again tip toe into the living room and tell her, "Yes, you are a virgin." Then another night when she again wakes up a sleeping family in the middle of the night, I realize I have to put my foot down. These middle of the night calls have been going on for almost three years, and I have to tell her something honestly. "Yes Rita, you are calling too late, and as you know I have three children in bed. You cannot phone me this late ever again. You cannot wake up an entire family." She seems to understand and apologizes. I suggest she write this down: "Don't wake up a sleeping family." She says she will write this on a piece of paper.

Two weeks later at 11:30 P.M. I answer the phone and it is the same question, but this time I decide on reverse psychology and turn the tables. I answer her question by telling her a story about John, a guy she dated when she was about 24 years old. "Rita, he had a huge crush on you." She listens. "This is during the time when you worked at City Hall in Porterville."

She replies, "I worked at City Hall?"

I say, "Yes. His nickname was *Big John* and you told me that you and *Big John* used to make out a lot and you loved kissing him."

She says, "I did?"

I continue, "Heck Rita, I wasn't with you every minute of every day girl, maybe you and *Big John* 'did it.' And if you did do it, then you are not a virgin."

Rita is shocked and says, "Really? I'm not? I don't remember this happening. Wouldn't I remember if we had sex? But I don't remember. I have no memory of having sex."

I tell her, "Maybe you're blocking it out. Now, it's almost midnight Rita, and time for you to go to bed and think about *Big John*."

Murray has no children. She's living alone when she receives the *Rita Enquiring* phone calls. She spends hours and hours talking to her, and tries to help her understand life's issues. Rita only wants to talk about sex. Murray is very patient; she is helpful, calm and logical, just as I have tried to be. Usually when Rita's calls come in though, I'm running on empty, and these midnight calls are making me crazy. Many times in the middle of the night, as I counsel Rita, I hear my oldest child get out of bed, the bathroom light flicks on, then he'll walk into the kitchen for water.

Murray tries with all she's got to help Rita understand, to help Rita remember and come to grips with her blank spots. I tell Murray how I changed up my answer so Rita will be satisfied and Murray replies, "Oh Banana, now she'll be hell-bent on trying to remember something that never happened, and she'll call us for the details." I am getting a short fuse from her never ending phone calls and questions, which are worded the exact same way each time. I change my answer so Rita will stop calling me in the middle of the night. But this idea backfires because she now wants to know more about sex, and what it's like.

I relay to her that I have no idea what her experience with sex was like; everyone has a different experience. "Rita, I wasn't there, and for all I know, you only kissed. So yes, there is a possibility that you're still a virgin."

She sadly replies, "Really?" We simply talk in circles for years and years and years. Rita is frustrated if she is a virgin and perplexed if she isn't.

Each time I answer, "Hello," her opening sentence is always verbatim: "Hi, Banana. I hope I'm not calling too late, but I need to ask you a question." But for her, it is the first time she's ever called, and it is the first time she builds up the courage to ask this personal question. This scenario continues until Rita is well into her late fifties. Murray and I continue to counsel Rita about this *issue* for thirty years.

Rita decides in the late 1980s that she has to meet a man and have sex. I yell through the receiver, "Rita, no!"

She asks innocently, "Why not?" I tell her in great detail about serial killers, mean men, abusive men, and pregnancy (you never know, Rita). I imagine and describe many other scenarios that could result from her picking up a stranger. Murray is also advising her to not get picked up and to not follow this plan; both Murray and I blast her with common sense and plead with her to calm down. I tell her instead to sit on her washing machine, on the spin cycle.

I laugh and she asks, "Why?"

"Oh, it's just an old joke, never mind."

One afternoon—during daylight hours—she phones. I'm naturally surprised as she catches me off guard. She announces that she's made up her mind and she is going out tonight, because tonight is the night. "Rita, NO! Please, do not pick up a guy, seriously Rita, you're gonna get hurt or injured. Really, no. I mean really hurt, Rita, physically hurt!"

She answers, "Good."

"You might get a disease," I say.

Rita says she has to do this and she'll tell me all about it. Then she adds, "And besides, you have sex, everyone has sex, why shouldn't I?"

"Well, for starters, you don't have a trusted mate."

And she replies, "I don't want a mate. I want sex."

I plead with her and warn her that I'm calling Murray. "Have you told Murray about your sex night planned for this evening?" Rita says she can't remember. Murray and I literally beg her to stay home. When the sun goes down and I tuck in my three children, my heart sinks.

I'm unable to fall into a restful sleep, waiting for a phone call that never happens. I'm so worried about her because she trusts people; she is innocent and vulnerable to the ways of the world.

The next day passes, and no call. Then, after the kids have their baths and are put to bed, I lie down and wait. It's about 11:00 P.M. when the phone rings. It's Rita; I thank her for calling at a decent hour, which really isn't a decent hour. "Rita dear, how are you? What happened with your plan to rape some unsuspecting man?"

This time, for the first time, she doesn't begin her call with the same worded question. This time she begins with, "Last night I met the nicest guy." Oh no, and I wait for the story.

Rita goes on to tell the tale of her evening of sex. "I met this guy at a bar. He was sitting at the bar and I was at a table, and he was a perfect gentleman. We had some drinks together and he asked me if I would like to go with him back to his apartment, and I did."

I'm thinking Oh boy, does she ever. I'm feeling scared, but urge her to continue. "Ok Rita, how did your evening of seducing this unsuspecting man turn out?" Now this story is interesting because she remembers every detail, and she can't seem to remember anything else. I guess her brain is on high alert.

Rita describes in detail how they walked into his studio apartment, he mixed another drink, and she sat on the edge of his bed, which was in the living room. She describes everything in the studio apartment and says to me, "Now Banana, this is the weird part. When we got to his place, he opened a window for fresh air. His place was really nice and clean. Then he walked over to me and laid me back on the bed."

"Go on," I urge.

"Well, he started kissing me, and he kissed my neck and my chest, then he laid on top of me and I looked at him straight in the eyes and said, 'Well, aren't you the big man about town.' Then Banana, he did the most confusing thing. He reared up on his arms and asked me what I'd just said, so I repeated it—'well aren't you the big man about town?' Then he looked at me, studied my face, then took his hand and rubbed the scar on my neck. He stood up, walked over to the kitchen, picked up the phone and called a cab company. I heard him tell the driver the address of the bar where my truck was parked. He turned around and told me that a taxi was on its way. Then he sat down next to me and said, 'It was nice meeting you. You are a very nice person, and you need to be careful.' When the taxi arrived, he walked me outside, and again he told me to be careful, and said 'Remember, it's not safe to pick up men.'"

Rita is confused and a little bit hurt because he abruptly called a taxi. But Murray and I know he had mistaken her slightly slurred speech for drunkenness. When he looked into her eyes he could see the vague look across them, the same look I'd noticed at my dad's house. He checked out the large scar at the base of her throat, then realized he'd picked up someone with a head injury and not an intoxicated woman.

I tell her how incredibly lucky she is. "And yes, Rita dear, he is a very nice man. So Rita, are you finished with this science project, and with this hormone induced notion of having sex?" She says she is, but she is perplexed and keeps asking what he saw in her that made him change his mind. She can't understand his concerns and his change of heart. I have to ask her, Well Rita, when you were in a passionate kiss, why did you berate him by asking if he was the big man about town? Why get sarcastic when this is what you've wanted for so many years?"

She replies, "I don't know."

Murray and I decide to drop it; let's leave her to stew for a while. She knows deep down inside that something went haywire. She is clearly disturbed and she wants to talk about it. She continues to tell us about how sad she felt as she looked out the cab window on her way back to her truck. This is very telling because she instinctively knows she's been rejected as a bed partner.

Murray and I talk about Rita's depression and decide to let her be, to give her space to work through her dream date fiasco. Our hearts ache for her; rejection is brutal. But when it's your first time out of the shoots and you're ready to experience a fantasy mixed with a passionate dream, and then you're rebuffed, well, this is a brutal blow to the inner hot Rita. She is the only one who can digest the results.

We're here if she needs us, but we friends are not going to rush back up to the green state of Oregon and hold her hand. Sometimes friends need to stay in the shadows and wait.

The man Rita chose as the one to deflower her is of noble character. Whoever you are—thank you.

> TO DESCRIBE MOTHER WOULD BE TO
> WRITE ABOUT A HURRICANE IN ITS PERFECT POWER.
>
> *Maya Angelou*

Kindling

RITA'S PATTERNED PATHS CONTINUE. The coming weekend will be a test of wills; Marie and Rita busy themselves to get their house in order. One of Marie's sisters is flying in to Eugene to spend a week, and they want everything perfect, in order, and in tip top shape. If it's her bossy Aunt Margaret, then they really need to get their act together. She will immediately notice if Marie and Rita are slacking. They vacuum the house, mop the kitchen, put dishes away, clean the cat box, mow the lawn, and make sure the bathroom is clean too. Marie prepares food and they wait. Marie keeps a nice home—it's not that they live in filth and disarray. Marie and Rita simply live comfortably, laid back. But when company stops by, they are cleaning machines.

Rita grabs her jacket and tells her mother she is going for a drive, as she does every evening, and she always ends up at the lumber yard.

Rita enjoys the task of gathering up kindling every evening, and this isn't a chore for her; it's her passion. Her bedroom is cleaned up and the sheets are changed, and off she goes, telling her Mozie she'll not stay out too late this night. The lumber yard is just a mile or two out of town and she's driven this road countless times.

It's closing time when Rita drives inside the gates, as always. The owner sees her and waves as he heads home for the night. He doesn't mind one bit if she helps herself to the kindling. He has grown fond of her evening visits. She pulls her pickup to the side of the old tin building next to the office then backs it towards a pile of discarded wood. She gets out and begins to collect certain pieces of discarded wood and tosses them into the truck bed. She is very picky and only wants certain sizes. Rita is oblivious to the two police cars that slowly drive down the long dirt driveway towards the wide gate leading into the lumber yard.

Rita continues to collect and toss wood, and when she looks up and sees the police, she just stands there. The police put on their red lights and park in a V so she can't get away. Rita drops her armload of kindling into the back of the truck and continues to wait in wonder. A policeman walks up to her and asks if her name is Rita Simpson.

She says, "Yes." Then he asks her, "Is this your vehicle?" and she says, "Yes." Next he reads her the Miranda Rights.

The policeman orders her to turn around, then he folds her over and across the hood of his police car as he handcuffs her behind her back. He escorts her to the side of the car and puts her in the backseat. I'm sure Rita thinks this is just plain crazy, but she must be scared and bewildered, too.

When Rita sits down in the back seat of the patrol car, the policeman slips into the driver's seat and stares at her from the vantage point of his rearview mirror. Rita stares back at his glare in the small slit of a mirror and states, "I didn't know it was against the law to collect kindling." He continues to stare back at her like she is a jokester punk and she continues to stare at him. Finally she belts out, "It's only kindling, for God's sake," and laughs nervously.

The police follow one another and drive her to the police station; they book her, finger print this dangerous thief, and take her mug shot. They tell her she can make one phone call. She says, "Well, thank you, Mister Nice Guy." It is 12:30 A.M. when she picks up the telephone and dials Mozie.

Marie and her sister are visiting as they wait for Rita. They're sitting by a roaring fire and have just poured their second highball when the phone rings. Rita tells her mother the most astonishing words: "Hi Mozie. I'm in jail."

Marie assumes Rita is joking, of course, and she asks, "Did you pass go and collect $200?"

Rita tells her mother, "No, really, I'm in jail. They just took my fingerprints with black ink, and they took my picture. When Rita says these words, they strike her as funny and she laughs out loud. This phone call takes longer than expected because Marie still thinks Rita is pulling a fast one. Finally she asks Rita what she'd done, and Rita confesses, "I collected two piles of kindling." Marie asks to speak to someone, thinking she'll hear, "Just kidding, Mozie," but instead Rita tells her to hold on.

Marie grabs her purse and Rita's medical files and runs out the door, leaving her sister to stoke the fire. She yells back to the house, "Gotta go bail out the kid." Rita waits in a private holding cell for her Mozie.

Marie walks into the police station with her usual swagger and I'm sure she wears a smirk, and her light blue eyes are flaming daggers. She knows she will prove them wrong and this she loves, the moment of winning. She meets with a policeman and asks him why they arrested her daughter, and what the charges were. "Rita has ongoing permission to pick up kindling and has been doing this for years," she explains. Marie goes on to tell the police about Rita's medical and health issues.

He snaps back that her daughter, Rita, has been robbing banks, and they have been tailing her for weeks. "We suspect she has the money stashed somewhere in the wood pile."

This is too much for Marie and she belts out a loud laugh. She quickly gathers her composure and explains to the officer about Rita's short term memory and her physical ailments from the violent car accident. She hands him Rita's medical file. They take Marie into a private office, but she balks and orders the release of her daughter immediately. He calls in a second policeman and they talk to Marie in a private, and explain that the girl robbing banks is tall, thin, and has short hair, she drives a small white pickup, and her name is Rita Simpson. Marie stares at the officer and tells him to release her daughter immediately or there will be consequences. "My daughter has never in her life stolen a penny. She is not the girl you are looking for, and there are plenty of white pickup trucks. My daughter is not capable of robbing a bank and hiding the money. She wouldn't remember where she stashed it anyway!"

Rita is finally released to her mother and they drive back home to visit with their company. The next day Marie and her sister drive into downtown Eugene and get Rita's impounded truck from the fenced-in area next to the police station. Later, Marie is paid back for any money they charged her, and Rita accepts their apology.

Oh to be a fly on the wall and listen to the sisters having a good stiff drink and visiting with Rita, the jail bird. Rita continues to insist she had permission, and questions, "Why is it against the law to pick up wood?" I don't understand why this is an issue if the owner said I could do it." She knows the situation is funny and odd, and she likes to listen to Marie explain why they arrested her.

This story is told and retold many times. Rita listens with a smirk and lunges forward to laugh. She refers to herself as *Robber Rita*. The real robber Rita Simpson was nabbed the following week. All of the above is on record and I wish Marie had kept the file with Rita's mug shot; this would be a classic photo.

The owner of the lumber yard also hears about the false arrest and mistaken identity, and he gets a good chuckle out of the story. Rita, arrested in his lumber yard—boy, would he love to have heard the conversation between her mother and the police.

A few months later Murray and I take a quick trip to Oregon to visit Rita; the first thing she asks us is to follow her so she can show us her kindling. She proudly opens the door that leads from the dining room into the sunken garage, and we step in.

One side is the usual garage stuff: old paint cans, yard tools, mower, and a wheel barrel. Murray and I sweep our visual to the other side of the garage; our eyes take in the sight of wonderment mixed with a little bit of sadness. Rita is an artist and she is obsessed with perfection-this we hadn't realized. The entire wall is stacked with kindling from floor to ceiling, from one side to the other in perfect order. Most of the wood is of medium color and stacked from the side door to the wide garage door. Her wall appears to be golden swirls of art, circles and lines. It is organized beyond your wildest imagination. Murray smiles and looks up and down and side to side. We stare. This wall is a wall of hundreds of golden swirls, a wall of art. It looks more like wall paper than stacked wood.

This is one of the few times my jaw drops and I am speechless. Finally I blurt out, "Wow Rita!" Murray is quiet and looks at the wall, then she tells our friend, "You've been a busy girl, Rita." Rita is very proud of this and she takes us outside to the side yard where she does her sorting. There we see various piles of wood. She shows us how she takes wood from this area to replace any wood she takes from the garage to use for fires. Every time she takes a piece out, she refills the stack with more. She is highly organized and has a meticulous operation going on. She shows us the tarp for rainy days and she shows us her hatchet.

We step back up and sit at the kitchen table. We ask for more details about the arrest. Marie is very smug about this event and gives us full details. Rita is not as scared as she is disturbed, because the police department has never returned the two piles of kindling she'd loaded into her pickup. My heart feels heavy as I listen. Murray says, "It sounds like the city owes you some wood, Rita." We try to make light if of it, but when Rita gets frustrated, she has a very hard time letting go. Marie nods yes in agreement; she has that look on her face, when she's thinking of something really wicked to say, but she holds her remark at bay. Rita looks angry, while the three of us nod in agreement.

A moment of silence lies across our table and we change topics. Marie states, "Well, my sister thoroughly enjoyed her visit." This makes us bust up laughing all together. Marie smirks.

The next day Rita drives us to the Willamette River and we toss skippers, walk along the river, and sit on the tail gate of her pickup and visit. Murray drives us to the hip downtown section of Eugene. We walk around and look at paintings, pottery, beadwork, and macramé. There are street musicians on every other corner and too many places to choose from when we get hungry. We look around at all of the healthy food cafés. We choose one, pop in, and eat healthy foods. The weather is breezy and cool, and we have a great time browsing, eating and walking around Eugene.

Rita hounds us about California. She nags us to move to Oregon, to get out of the heat and the dryness and away from the crowds of people; she only sings praises for Oregon. We have to agree-this is a beautiful town. We wander into a sports store and I buy my sons t-shirts that have art work in yellow and green across the chest and say, "Oregon Ducks." I buy my daughter a popup book and myself a necklace. We sit in the courtyard in the shopping plaza by a fountain and eat ice cream. Rita wants to show us the new building for the Green Hill Humane Society.

We patiently listen to her repeated stories and we tell her how much we love the new building, how much we love the lumber yard, and how beautiful and green the area is around Eugene. "You're lucky to live in this area," we say.

Elephant in the room: it's interesting to us that miss Midnight Caller Rita never once brings up the subject of her virginity while we're there. When we're home, we get calls from her about two or three times a week with intense conversations on this subject. We talk for long periods of time and try to help her process her ongoing urge to find the answer. Yet, face to face with us—*the Answer Girls*, Rita never once mentions this subject. We dare not bring up the late night calls. Murray and I decide it is probably more like phone sex, so we smile and keep it to ourselves. She probably doesn't have the nerve to talk about this private subject with both of us, together, at the same time, face to face.

We give our friend a nice big hug goodbye. We hug Mombo and tell her she can bail us out anytime. She smirks in agreement and gives Rita a nudge using her shoulder. Back in the car, we wave goodbye to our friend who always seems to get into bizarre situations. "Bye now, until next time."

A TRUE FRIEND KNOWS THE SONG IN MY HEART AND
SINGS IT TO ME WHEN MY MEMORY FAILS.

DONNA ROBERTS

Tennis Balls and Apples

RITA PHONES ONE MORNING, *yes morning,* and says she is driving to my house to visit for a few days. My jaw drops. "Rita, what are you thinking! I live a six hour drive away; how will you ever find me? Once you get to Chico, my house is located in a maze of streets."

Marie picks up the phone and says, "Rita has your address. I can get her as far as the Red Bluff exit, off I-5. Just give me directions past Red Bluff. So I carefully give Marie the easiest way to find Chico. She tries to comfort me by saying, "Rita has a map and she'll draw a line as I tell her directions." I am still nervous. Then Marie tells me, "Banana, Rita has to do this trip. She wants to drive alone and she wants to visit you and your family. She will use file cards and will check them as needed. The kid will be fine." Uh, file cards? I think. I can't imagine what that means, but decide not to ask.

She's to arrive on a Friday. I'm very nervous and tense and worried. Jeff is very excited, as he remembers Rita and likes her. I look out my kitchen window 500 times this day. Dana and Spencer stand on a wooden step stool so they can keep watch out the dining room window for mommy's friend. Jeff runs home from school and waits with us. The clock ticks by as we wait for a phone call, something, anything that gives us an idea of her whereabouts. I remember back to her last visit to Chico and it crosses my mind that some things never change; here I am, waiting for Rita.

Our home is a in a maze of homes and very difficult to locate, even for locals. Many friends report driving in circles to try and find us. It is getting late in the afternoon when I look up again, out of habit, just in time to see a little white pickup with a new camper shell pull up right in front of our house. "She's here!" I yell to the kids.

We run out to see her and Jeff grabs her duffel bag. She doesn't seem tired one bit. She is smiling and says, "Wow, Jeff, you've really grown," and "This must be little Spencer," and "Oh Lollie, aren't you cute." Spencer stands there on the lawn in his overalls with a Viking sword. Dana holds back with shyness and smiles. Rita doesn't care about coming in; she prefers to stand on the lawn and talk to the kids, and she does. Then, finally, I ease her into the house and she continues to talk to the kids with great joy.

We have a nice dinner, then the kids have their baths and put on their pajamas. I continue to show Rita their rooms and toys. I tell Rita that I have to go to a meeting at the school concerning a yearly fund raiser we have called The County Fair. I have a booth and I'm also on a committee for decorating. "I'll be right back," I tell her. "It'll be about thirty or forty five minutes. Can you please stay with the kids?" She says she would love to, and my three kids clap with joy.

Now looking back on this as an older adult, I have to wonder, what was I thinking?

I discreetly ask Jeff to help Rita and he says he will. I trust him because he's almost eleven and he instinctively knows she is not an actual adult, she just looks like one. The kids say they'll behave, and Jeff announces that he will be the boss of Rita. Rita belts out a laugh. She assures me everything will be fine, and not to worry. "No one likes a worried Banana," she asserts.

Jeff asks, "What's a worried Banana?" Ah, Jeff I'll explain later.

I return home forty minutes later. I unlock the front door and Jeff calls out, "Mom, we're in here and we need help!" Oh my God. I dash into Jeff's bedroom and there's Rita, on the top bunk, stuck. Her arm is caught between the bed and the wall. Spencer is up there with her, holding a jar of Vaseline. Dana is on the floor holding her pink stuffed elephant, watching with a grin like this is an episode of Scooby Doo or something. Jeff has a screw driver and is attempting to dismantle the bunk beds.

"Jeff, stop. Everyone, stop," I say. Spencer climbs down like a little monkey. I look up to Rita and ask her, "What happened? Are you ok?"

She yells down to me, "They wanted to show me their new bunk beds!" Between Rita and Jeff, the picture emerges. Apparently Jeff had crawled up, and Spencer followed. In scooting over to make room for Rita, Spencer got his leg stuck. So Rita climbed up and reached in to get his leg out. Spencer fairly easily pulled his leg out, but then Rita's arm got stuck in the same spot.

The rest of the story I put together on my own. Spencer tries to free Rita by greasing up her elbow, and Jeff thinks dismantling the bed will fix everything, since he's too weak to move the bed with Rita on it. Rita laughs like a hyena, Jeff and Spencer are all smiles, and Dana and the pink elephant watch with wide-eyed innocence from the floor. I'm the only one who realizes that if Jeff's problem solving idea had been a success, the bed would have come crashing down with Rita on it. It's a good thing I got here when I did.

Together, Jeff and I are able to pull the bed away from the wall and free Rita's arm. She rubs her sore arm and climbs down. Spencer hands me the jar of Vaseline. I ask him for the lid, too, but we discover it is hopelessly unreachable behind the heavy bunk beds. We get everyone to settle down and all the kids are giggling and happy. Rita says she's sorry about the bed and I make sure her arm isn't injured. She shows it to me and says, "It's just a little red and swollen by my elbow." Then she adds, "I was on the top bunk the whole time you were gone." Oh good lord Rita, I think. Spencer is consumed with ace bandages and wraps Rita's injury from her wrist to her upper arm. She laughs, thanks him, and keeps it on all night. I tell her how sorry I am. She replies, "Its ok, Banana, you have great kids, and I had a lot of fun." Rita has a beautiful smile on her face and she seems genuinely happy.

My husband Don comes in from work at his usual 9:15. He says hi to Rita, welcomes her to our home, and asks her about the trip down. The kids rush in and tell him their crazy bunk bed story. He goes in and tightens up the screws on the bed and pushes it back against the wall. He comes out of the room holding the Vaseline lid and looks at me questioningly. "Don't even ask," I say.

Rita's happy-tired and all three kids are cheerful and full of energy. But off to bed they go. The boys get in their newly reinforced bunks, Jeff on top, Spencer on the bottom. Dana crawls into our bed. Rita falls into a restful sleep in Dana's twin bed under her pink billowing canopy and matching pink bed spread.

The next day after breakfast I ask Rita if she'd like to walk with me to Pleasant Valley High School and hit some tennis balls. I secretly hope this activity will help jolt her memory since she had been on the tennis team with Murray.

The kids watch Saturday morning cartoons with their dad. We grab two tennis rackets and two cans of balls and off we go. We walk the few blocks to the high school, jaywalking when necessary, and cross the track and the football field to get to the tennis courts. There are three large flat white back boards on a paved asphalt area. I figure she can practice hitting tennis balls on the backboard. The weather is great and Rita is ready to go; let's practice!

She hits the first ball so hard it soars over the backboard and lands in a cyclone fenced area for the high school agriculture class. Ball two, wham, over the top and into the fenced in area. I yell over to her, "Don't hit the ball so hard, Rita. Don't hit it over the wall, hit it dead center in the middle of the white wall like this, see?" I show her how it's done. Ball three, wham. Ball four, wham. Ball five, wham. "No! You're hitting it too hard!" I yell. "Let's hit the ball to each other instead, ok?" So I gently serve the ball to her, it bounces once, and she steps in and scoops it up with her racket like a professional and whams it over the backboard behind me. Her ball looks like a green jet flying over my head. We use up the rest of the balls in the same way: I hit a ball to her, she slams it over the top and into the fenced in area. Finally, my temper rises. "Rita, you emptied both cans! Now crawl over that fence and YOU pick up all the tennis balls, Miss Muscles!"

She cheerfully says, "Ok," and laughs as she happily walks to the backside of the backboard. There in the enclosure are apple trees, and on the ground are apples and tennis balls in the same shade of green. I point this out to Rita, and she says, "I'll get the balls. Do you want any apples?" I suggest she only pick up the balls, and leave the apples alone.

I plunk my bottom down on the grass and watch as she begins her ascent over the cyclone fence. After a moment or two, this scene strikes me as funny. I begin to laugh because it is so ridiculous, and so wrong. It really is laughable. I'm watching her and I think to myself, What have I done? She has a head injury and I'm making her climb a cyclone fence. My laughter grows uncontrollable and makes me rock back and forth just as she mounts the top of the fence. There she sits, balancing with one leg on each side of the fence as if she's sitting on a horse. I wail with laughter and choke with joy. Rita looks down at me and watches me with a curious expression on her face. Her gaze and this entire scene make me laugh even harder. With tears running down my cheeks, I have to slap my knees.

Finally she speaks in a very matter-of-fact voice. She says, "I remember you. I remember you used to laugh all the time. We used to drive around a lot. You left me stranded once. And we're friends."

Rita, perched on top of a cyclone fence, experiences a total recall, a moment of clarity. I jump up, still laughing with red eyes, and yell up to her, "Yes! Yes, Rita, yes!" She goes on, still wanting to tell what she remembers. She remembers us laughing together.

She comes back to the present and says, "Look at me. Why am I sitting up here, you dip wad? Why did you make me get up here?" Hearing her dry wit, I begin to wail again and fall back down to the grass with pure joy. Ha! She calls me out and she calls me a name. I love it. Oh, how I've missed this part of her.

Looking up to her I yell, "You're supposed to get the balls you hit into the mini apple orchard, you Bionic Woman! Now jump down and toss me the balls, and I'll put them back in the cans." Rita jumps down, but as she does, the bottom of her blouse gets hooked on the top of the fence and when she lands, her blouse pulls off over her head and outstretched arms. Now Rita is standing inside the caged orchard in nothing but her pedal pushers, Keds and bra. I fall down to my knees and almost pee my pants, she looks so funny. As I'm roaring with laughter, I turn and see something I hadn't noticed before. Oh, Judi! I think to myself. I blurt, "Rita, you're going to kill me, but there's a gate over there and it's unlocked." She makes a very snotty remark as she buttons up her blouse, and tries to stifle a laugh. I run around to the side, push open the gate, and together we begin to sift through the green apples and balls, tossing balls over the fence as we find them. When we exit the enclosure to collect the balls and put them back in the cans, I notice Rita's blouse is full of apples. Giggling, we walk together across the fresh cut grass.

My happiness is obvious and Rita continues to reflect and describe many things she remembers from our past. This is a joyous day. I ask her if she remembers the times I slept at her house and she quickly replies, "You used to take a bubble baths."

I skip along with her and say, "Rita, do you remember the peeping Tom outside your bedroom window?"

She says, "Now you're making this up."

"No, seriously, Rita. We used to hear the bushes moving and we'd lay real still and we knew he was out there. Then one night, I was changing into my pajamas and this idiot stood so close to the screen, I could see his face; his nose was about to touch the screen! What a moron. He assumed he was protected in the shadows, I guess. I pretended not to see him, then I screamed to you, 'He's at the window!' Rita, you were in the kitchen and you bolted out your back kitchen door and chased him back to his house. It turned out he was your neighbor; his house was directly behind your garage. Do you remember? The funny thing is you used to warn me to stay away from his older brother because he was crazy, but this one was watching us!"

Rita's expression begins to fade. I can tell I'm over stimulating her with these stories. I mention Hag Hollow and she only smiles. I mention GaGa's Go and how much fun we had in that car. Rita seems to be with me, still in the now, but she is too tired to respond. Together we walk along the sidewalk in the warm late morning sun, and we're back on track. I want to run ahead of her and walk backwards so we can continue to talk, but I force myself to calm down. Rita looks tired so we transfer all the apples from her blouse into the cup of my t-shirt.

She's tired from her long drive, tired from being pinned to the top bunk with my children, tired from hitting tennis balls into outer space, and tired from scaling a cyclone fence. After a period of silence, she calmly tells me she remembers my laugh, our hair blowing in her car, and my mother. "She's real short, isn't she?" she asks.

"Yes she is, Rita. She's only 4'11." With a happy sigh we walk, she is clearly content, and a thousand stories want to burst out.

I remind her about the time she and Tish took a road trip and the following weekend came to visit me in Bakersfield. "You two had stopped at that place on highway 99 where there's a big blinking hand on the side of the road." Everyone knows that place. I continue, "You and Tish went in and had your palms read. Do you remember this Rita?"

She replies "I didn't get my palm read."

"Yes, you did. The palm reader told you that you'd meet a handsome Italian man and marry him and live in a grape vineyard in Italy and have three children and live to be in your 80s. I think she must have been hitting the vino herself, before your visit."

This story makes Rita throw her head back and let out a big laugh. "Ok," she says, "I guess I can live in a vineyard."

I say, "Rita, because of you and Tish, I decided to stop there too."

"No you didn't," she counters.

"Oh yes I did. The fortune teller told me I had a wall up between me and men. And for eighty dollars she'd help me over the wall." Rita laughs so hard I think she's going to pee her pants like I did back at the apple trees. We walk into the house still laughing.

"Rita, do you remember the time we bought matching outfits to go to the Springville rodeo?"

She looks at me and asks, "Why would we do that?"

"Because we both liked the material," I tell her. "It was green and blue specks, a tweed."

She asks, "What's tweed?" "It's like your sofa; tiny bumpy knobby material," I tell her.

We sit and talk and I encourage her to try and remember. In the dining room I inform her, "Rita, it was Freddy who called me the day of your accident to tell me what had happened and how to contact your mother."

She seems surprised and replies, "He did?" I pour us a glass of water. The kids come into the room and she talks to them, gulps water, then looks my way and asks, "Who's Freddy?" I tell her the short version, which is that I had a huge crush on him, and she says, "Oh, yes. I remember him. I don't think I liked him because you liked him."

I remind her about the time he asked if she could give him a ride from Snow White drive-in to Coleman's drive-in, which was at the other end of the drag where we turn around to drive back and forth. "You hesitated, but I said, 'Sure, climb in.' And then to you I said, 'All he wants is a ride to his car—it's no big deal.'" I continued the story. "The latch on your Healy passenger door was not working very well, remember? And when we drove around I had to hook my arm over the door to help it stay in the *click* position. If I didn't, the latch could've opened. So Freddy squished into the front seat with us, but he didn't know to hold the door. You slowed down for the light on the corner of Olive and Main, then you floor boarded your Healy and the door instantly fell open and Fred fell right out the door. He caught himself by holding onto the door, and his legs stayed inside, but his torso went right down onto the street." Rita's been listening intently and she busts up laughing. She obviously likes this story. I go on, "He pulled himself back up into the car and laughingly asked, 'Are you trying to kill me, Rita?' And you said, 'That's not a bad idea.'" Rita's mouth falls open and she says she can't believe she said such a thing.

I step into the kitchen to make a snack; she and the kids go in the open family room. Rita is happy. In a few minutes, she walks over to me at the kitchen sink, looks straight at me and asks, "Who's Freddy?"

Again I tell her he is a friend from our hometown. "You didn't like him much, but I did."

It clicks, and she says, "Oh, oh, yes, I remember him now. Right. I remember." I begin toasting strawberry Pop Tarts for everyone, two at a time, so it takes a while. She and I talk about our next adventure for the day.

"You wanna visit my mom?" I ask.

Rita likes this idea, smiles, then looks at me as I hand her a plate with a pop tart and asks, "Who's Freddy?" Once again I explain, and five minutes later, "Who's Freddy?" She asks me this question, with the same wording, every five minutes for a full hour. My heart sinks.

Jeff whispers to me, "Why does she keep asking you who Freddy is and you tell her and she forgets?" I explain that she had a terrible car accident when she was a young woman and she hit her head, so sometimes she forgets the answers. Jeff somehow understands. He sticks close to her and tells her things about our home and is ready for any repeated questions.

Rita has gone down the hall to the bathroom, and when she walks back out and up the hall to where I am, she asks me, "Who's Freddy?" At this point I have to stop her because she's just on auto pilot and can't stop asking the same question.

I say, "Rita, you have asked this same question too many times now, Dear, and I've explained it to you each time. You need to stop asking because it doesn't matter. There are so many other things in life that matter."

She listens and seems to understand. After apologizing, she waits a few minutes and asks, in a very innocent voice, "Who's Freddy?"

Jeff steps up and tells her rather assertively, "He's Mom's friend." And she stops.

Rita goes into our bedroom and lays down to take a nap. While she rests, I make an apple pie, with the help of four additional very tiny hands. Later Rita enjoys dinner with all the kids around the table jabbering, because she's a child herself. Soon after the kids go to bed, we follow along. It's been a long day.

My Dear Rita leaves the next morning to drive back to her home in Eugene. Her presence in my home causes each room she's in to be full of warmth and love, and this surrounds me and my children. She feels like a sister to me. I admire her courage and her resilience; she never gives up trying to learn. I walk her out to her truck and notice something on her dashboard. It's a stack of three by five cards, each with a specific direction on it. This is how she made her way from Oregon to California; she tells me she pulls over and reads a card, follows the direction on it, then pulls over to read the next one. After each card is used, she places it at the bottom of the stack and takes off again. Marie must have taught Rita this method of memory from her days as a librarian.

Now, she will be driving back home. She looks at her white card and places it under the stack. Oh, how I hope she doesn't turn a corner too fast making her cards slide off the dashboard. But she is prepared. She has each card numbered just in case this happens. She is not worried one bit about the drive home.

Her repetitive questions can make a person crazy, no doubt, and I have tried to be patient and answer the same questions over and over again. Her visit is very positive overall. We do visit my mother and Rita seems to remember her. My children love Rita, and they beg me to let her babysit again someday. This innocent request makes me smile.

I hate to see her pull away from our curb. We stand there on the sidewalk; Spencer and Dana are holding my hands, and Jeff stands next to the curb, as close he can get without getting his foot run over. I wonder if he might jump in the truck with her as she drives by, but he just waves goodbye. She flips a U-turn and waves her arm out the window like I've seen her do a thousand times.

From the day she opened her eyes after a four month coma, it takes Rita eight years to remember me. Well, eight years and watching me have a laughing fit from the vantage point of a seven-foot fence. This moment is very special and rewarding for both of us, and it stays with me forever. It makes me realize that with Rita—or maybe anyone with a head injury—you can tell her your shared memories a hundred times and they won't stick. But as soon as she lives it again, as soon as she's actually in the role of best friend again, all the memories become real. This new knowledge helps me understand Rita's behavior from years ago at the county fair. Rita tagged along with the friends she didn't really remember. But as soon as she saw Burger's bent over butt in the context of a county fair booth, with all its rich sights and smells, it was a moment of friendship and familiarity. Whack went the cane, and good ol' ornery Rita was back, if only for a few minutes.

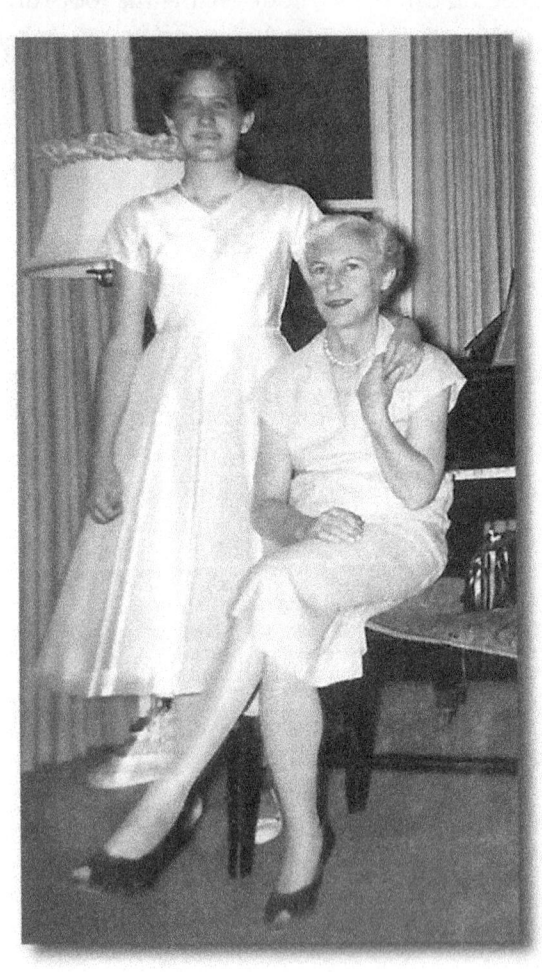

> FRIENDS SHOW THEIR LOVE
> IN TIMES OF TROUBLE, NOT IN HAPPINESS.
>
> *Euripides*

Mozie

MURRAY PHONES ONE MORNING and says she heard rumors that Marie is in the hospital. When Murray tells me, I think back to Marie and it's no surprise that she suffers from emphysema—she always has a *ciggy* between her lips.

1988

Seems to me, reflecting back, Marie wasn't smoking the last time we visited, and Murray says she quit years before. I thought she'd cut back because of Rita's breathing issues due to her punctured lungs from the car accident. I wonder now if she stopped smoking on doctor's orders. Marie never showed signs of distress or crazy joy. She was a mystery woman. *Steady Eddie*—the same—no matter what.

Rita's Road

Murray and I hem haw around and she says she'll see about working out her schedule so we can drive up and check out the situation. "You have any time in the near future that will work for you to get a clean get away, Nana? If not this week, how about the following week? Or the next? What do you think about those bananas, Banana?" She and I ponder the calendar, as we figure we have lots of time to make a decision. I tell her I actually think I can work it out with clients and my schedule, and it will be easier if we drive up on a Friday. Then the kids could be with their dad after school and through the weekend. We decide to talk in a couple of days, and agree we need to jam up there and show our support for our gal Rita, who must be out of her mind with worry, and alone.

It works out for us to drive up the very next Friday, much sooner than we hoped. Murray drives north from the Santa Cruz Hills to my house. She must have been up with the chickens because she makes it to my house by late morning. I've moved and now live in a small country town called Durham, just a few miles from Chico. Murray, the professional stalker, has found me. I show her around my new house, the kids' bedrooms, the kitchen, and the acre. We eat and prepare for a very long drive, and off we go, another road trip.

We drive for a couple of hours and stop in Mt. Shasta, a tiny hippie mountain town with fresh crisp air and a huge mountain as the back drop. Murray and I discovered Mt. Shasta on one of our trips north to Eugene in the late 1970s. On our last trip there, we stumbled onto this little hideaway café located on a side street off Mt. Shasta Blvd. We step inside to another world, buy freshly made bagels, cream cheese, two bottles of water, and other snacks. Soon we are back on the road with our food in brown paper bags waiting to be devoured.

We talk all the way, mostly about our lives, the decisions we've made whether good or bad, and we talk about our careers. We talk about Rita, and what might happen if and when Marie does pass on, and how this will impact Rita's future. We don't think we'll live to see this happen and we have all kinds of ideas and bad scenarios. We both agree it's a good thing we're taking this trip, if only to be there to show our support during this very scary time.

"I didn't know Marie was ill. Did you, Murray?"

"No, not really. She was always the same: sarcastic with a slight smile. She was very hard to read."

I relate to Murray, "In the beginning, when I first met Marie, I didn't know if she'd scold me for cleaning out her ash tray, or serve me a homemade meal. But as the years passed by, I could read her smirk, smile or wide grin."

Murray agreed, saying, "If Marie didn't like you, she'd leave the room. If she liked you, she'd give you her two cents with a smirk."

"Yeah, I noticed her coughing now and then, but I suppose that's expected from a smoker. I hope she returns home while we're still there this weekend. That way we can force feed her some healthy foods."

We stop along the Rouge River to rest and use the facilities. We get out, stretch and walk to a side area and find a spot secluded from everything except the cab of a huge truck. We unfold our bags of food that we'd hoarded from Mt. Shasta and begin to have lunch on an old wooden picnic table not far from a wooden bridge next to a nice flowing creek. We eagerly dive into our bagels. I remember noticing the truck cab when we walked by heading to the rest rooms; it's parked not far from our table, and we had to climb down five well-worn handmade steps to find this woodsy area. Still, this spot seems private with fresh clean air and the sound of the creek.

But the large cab without a trailer keeps me on my usual high alert. I begin to wonder where the driver is and what he's up to; it just sits there, as if the driver is waiting to pick up a pod, or he's heading home after his delivery, or he might tow something. We guess the driver pulled over and is trying to catch up on his sleep. At first we are oblivious to the big truck cab, even though it stands out like an elephant; we are more interested in searching for a table and eating. But I'm wired to notice when something is out of place.

Murray is relaxed and she pulls off more string cheese and munches on crackers and smears cream cheese on our bagels and opens our water. I notice the antenna is beginning to sway back and forth, so I tell Murray to turn around and look behind her. She turns around and notices this very familiar rhythm as the antenna begins to move faster and faster. Oh no, they're having sex in the cab of his truck!

Murray groans, "Ah f***. Let's get out of here." We look at the antenna and try to stifle our laughter; it's really goin' to town. She says, "Ahhh, seriously! Come on 10-4 good buddy, already!" We grab our food and water bottles and run up the steps past the front of his cab, and all the way to Murray's car. We jump in and Murray yells, "If the cab's rockin' don't bother knockin!" She spins out, leaving a screen of dust balls and a trail of scattering rocks behind us.

We cruise north on I-5 munching in her car, dropping sesame seeds with every bite. Each of us wears a painted smile of cream cheese on our lips. I'm addicted to these wonderful road trips, with no hint of stress or life's hassles. There's nothing better than cruising with an old friend and enjoying the reconnection, whether we talk or not. I say, "It is such a long drive to Eugene, and I have to pee again, but I'll hold it. I don't want to see another trucker doing the horizontal bop."

Murray advises me to stop drinking so much water. "It's a simple science equation Nana; what goes in must come out."

I'm feeling tired, but it is much worse for Murray, who has already tackled the Bay Area traffic early this morning, then veered off towards Chico to pick me up, then back on I-5 again. Finally we're getting closer and the landscapes are greener and lush.

Murray parks in the driveway on Camelot Street; it's about 4:00 P.M. Bill, Rita's brother, walks across the lawn to greet us. He walks towards the car, bends over to look inside the driver's side window, and we're just about to yell, Hey Bill, we made it, when Bill quietly says, "Marie died an hour ago."

It is spooky for us to be this close in timing. And how did this happen? We didn't know she was so bad, so close. We ask how Rita is holding up, and he says she blames the doctor for killing her mother. Oh dear, I can just imagine. We wonder, is it inappropriate for us to go in, or should we back out and go home? Bill must be able to read our expressions and he graciously invites us to come in and have some snacks. "Rita will love to see you two," he says. Murray and I are shocked and saddened by this unexpected news and, frankly, at a loss for words.

We sit there in Murray's car for a minute to collect our thoughts. We haven't prepared for this and we're not sure what to do. We didn't know Marie was gravely ill, or that her illness had advanced to this point. She has just died and we're in her driveway. It's amazing and weird at the same time. We're kind of in a state of disbelief.

"Poor Rita," I say.

Murray replies, "Join the crowd. Well Tex, we might as well go inside. I'm sure Rita could use our support."

We quietly knock on the front door not knowing what to expect, and Murray slowly pushes the door open. We see a very small group of people. Bill and his family are sitting at the dining room table, and a lovely Asian woman, who lives next door, is there. She has always been very good to Rita and her mother. I sit down in the same wing back chair Marie pinned a note on when she played a practical joke, and scared me out of my wits. Murray sits on the couch next to me. We look at each other and decide, with our ESP eyeball communication, to bolt and walk down the hall. The house is eerily quiet.

Rita's in her bedroom sitting on her twin bed, and Murray knocks lightly on the door. Rita asks, "Who's there?" Then, without waiting for an answer, she tells the stranger to come in. Murray peeks through the crack in the slightly open door and looks towards Rita. Rita must recognize Murray's one big blue eye peering through the opening of the door and says, "What are you doing here? How did you know?" We step in and go straight to Rita, who has swollen red eyes. We each give her a big hug and tell her how much we loved her Mozie, and how sorry we are.

Bill and Genia seem to be in quiet disbelief also. I'm certain Rita's care is of most concern to them. Marie's death was swift, and no one really knows what to do.

Rita keeps asking us how we knew. She states the facts. "It just happened—Mozie just died. We just got back home from the hospital and you two walk in. This is weird as hell."

Now this sounds more like our old Rita. So we explain our arrival as honestly as we can: "We're psychic."

We ask Rita if she wants to take a drive and she agrees, but only if she drives. Murray tells her to get in the passenger's seat and relax. Off we go, out into the countryside. We drive along a beautiful creek, up into the hills and around a neighborhood, past the same ol' lumber mill and past the same Green Hill Humane Society where Rita spends so much of her time. Rita needs to do this and she needs time to grieve. We ask her if she wants us to stay or leave, and she says, "Yes, please stay." We drive to the Willamette River, walk across manicured lawns to the rocky shore, and stand by the river's edge to look at the wide river and moving water. Normally we would toss skippers, but not today. We just stand and look, the three of us. Eventually we drive back to Camelot Street.

When we walk in, Bill announces to Murray, "Since you and Banana are such good friends, we're putting you two in the front bedroom in a double bed."

"Well, sure, ok, why not?" we stammer. Murray and I have never slept together, well, except for camping.

Dinner is over and we visit with Rita and make sure she's not too overwhelmed with grief. We also make sure she stays home. We remove her car keys off the hutch just to make sure. Our worries are all for naught; Rita is very tired and she wants and needs to grieve privately.

We brush our teeth, put on our flannel pajamas and say goodnight to Rita. We turn out her lights and she lies down in her bed. Murray and I are both relieved that we're here to be with her at this time. We stew over this and hope our presence adds a tiny shred of comfort.

Murray is in charge of the lights in our room. She asks me if I'm ready, then she clicks and runs and jumps into bed and joins me under the covers. We both, at the same time, adjust the quilts and fluff them up and down so they are flush and have no wrinkles. Then each of us lays straight, arms at our sides, legs together. Murray doesn't move a muscle, nor do I, for a long while. We are stiff soldiers, frozen in bed. We chat a little bit about our bad timing, or unusually perfect timing. Then we close our eyes and wait for sleep to take over, or so I assume. I won't move for fear she'll think I'm snuggling up to her and hurt me. But Murray seems to be out cold.

It is after one o'clock in the morning now, and I decide that Murray is dead. She hasn't moved a muscle, not even her big toe, since we said goodnight. I can't even hear her breathing. My hand moves slowly from my side and my fingers begin to walk a few inches, between the sheets, towards her right leg. Ever so gently I touch her leg with my finger to see if she is stiff and cold, and generally to check if rigormortis has set in. When I barely touch her leg she snaps, "Get your hand off my leg. What the hell are you doing?" I let out a chicken cackle and she asks me if I have a problem.

Choking back a laugh I tell her "I thought you were dead and I had to check; it's my job because I don't have any desire to sleep with a corpse." Murray lets out a laugh and confesses she considered that I might be dead too. We giggle for a while, those quiet giggles you do when you're in a library. Finally sleep lays her hands on our eyes, and before you know it, the sun is up.

Next day we keep a low profile; we visit Rita, sit on her bed and talk about nothing, and everything. I look at the wall next to her bed and happily notice the decoupage I made for her so many years ago. Hanging next to the 70s art is Andy's painting of a panda bear, one of her first pieces. To help her remember us, Rita has these bits of memorabilia. I think about what physical item I have from Marie. My mind goes back to the time at Hag Hollow when I notice a box of worn but nice pieces of finished oak. At the bottom of the weathered box, I see pieces of iron, for the mechanics of what, I don't know. It turns out they are parts for an old oak stool from the Porterville City Library. It's one stool from a set of only two. Mombo sees me digging in the box of oak and I ask her what her plans are for the wood. "Firewood," she says, "unless you want it." I can't let these vintage pieces of oak be fed to a fire. My husband picks up the box and puts it in the back of our car, rescuing it from pyromaniac Mombo. He painstakingly puts it all back together. Marie is shocked when I tell her how beautiful the rebuilt stool is; she didn't even think all the pieces were there. The vintage stool becomes a part of my home furnishings for years to come. I still have it today, sitting at our kitchen counter, waiting for buns to warm it up.

My mind returns to Rita's room, where Murray and I decide to get Rita away from the quietness of her home for a while. We take her to breakfast, then for a nice long ride. A full tummy and a drive are very soothing to the soul. But this time she surprises us when she says she wants to go back home. Once there, her brother wants to talk to her about finances and spending, which we all know are out of control. There is obvious tension in the air, but we don't connect it to Rita and Bill. We have no idea how much Rita is spending, but her freedom is about to come to a screeching halt. And Rita will surprise us all with her will of iron, her resources, and her determination.

Murray tells me that Rita likes to gamble, and if she ever finds a black jack table, she's in. Bill has to put a stop to her behavior with no consequences. We figure Bill is going to lower the boom and we don't want to be around when it comes down.

Rita doesn't say much, but she alludes to the fact that Marie's doctor killed her. We don't respond with a lot of emotion. We let it go and let her vent. Murray and I both know that when Rita gets a notion, she's like a dog with a rag in its mouth; she'll never be the one to stop tugging.

We sit at the table and have some coffee and talk about Marie. We have all sorts of stories and, well, mine is cleaning out her cigarette butts and getting a lecture at the tender age of 14. Her deal is, she used to pick through the butts in her ashtray, find one long enough, and re-smoke it. I recall her home on Grand Avenue; they had a baby grand piano, imported china sitting in an imported hutch waiting for special occasions, and there were many books and highly stimulating conversations there. But when Marie went to bed, she'd flop down on a roll away bed and slip into a sleeping bag. Marie was raised in a home with strict rules, style and class. To me she was one big bag of mixed signals, an oxymoron of life. Nothing made any sense, and as a young impressionable girl I was mesmerized by her.

She had such a beautiful face—tiny sharp features, short wavy white hair, piercing blue eyes, thin lips and a tiny figure. I didn't understand her and never will, not then, not now. I have never since, and probably never will come across the likes of Marie. She always dressed down, casual, plain and understated. She kept quiet in a crowd and she rarely fully smiled. She wore a half smile, which was sexy. I just didn't understand what made her tick. I've thought of her for many years, and even now.

Murray has many stories of Marie too, and one is the egg in the refrigerator. Neither Marie, GaGa nor Rita knew if the egg was raw or boiled, so Marie went into the kitchen with an ink pen, wrote the date on the mystery egg, and set it back in the refrigerator. And there it sat for the next nine years.

Murray also said Marie edited children's books and traveled around the United States with the author. Marie was brilliant.

I remember a time when Rita and I, in our young teens, play the Ouija board and it leads us to spell out a name. We say the letters aloud, then put it together as a name. Marie turns her head and looks at us from the kitchen and asks, "What did you just spell?" and we spell this name again. This is the one and only time I am a witness to Marie being totally flabbergasted. She says, "You just said the name of my great grandmother."

Marie's face is flushed and she asks us if we made that up and we say, "No. It just went to the letters, really." Rita tells her mother she didn't know her great great grandmother's name. It's really spooky, and I can clearly remember every detail. We were sitting at the corner of the long dining room table, next to the kitchen.

All friends loved Rita's mother. Who wouldn't? She was quiet and very cool, non-intrusive. She put no curfew or boundaries on her daughter or her friends. She edited books, worked at the City Library, and she helped students and writers. But on weekends she was a different person. She loved to camp, play board games and card games, travel, and she passionately enjoyed nature. If ever there was a mother who was needed to live a very long full life, it was Marie, Rita's safety net. Marie could have been a survivalist out in the wild.

During this time of loss is when Rita begins to refer to her mother as "my little Mozie." With Mozie gone, everything changes, and especially for Rita because her mother was her anchor, her trusted friend, her memory and her Mozie. Marie had developed X-ray vision and she knew when Rita needed help and when Rita needed freedom. She was the dial on her daughter's compass.

The next part of Rita's life will be very interesting and terrible to watch. Camelot Street will never be the same.

> OUR BROTHERS AND SISTERS ARE THERE WITH US
> FROM THE DAWN OF OUR PERSONAL LIVES,
> TO THE INEVITABLE DUSK.
>
> Susan S. Merrell.

Money Matters

BILL AND RITA HAVE TO TALK ABOUT MONEY. Marie left her house on Camelot Street to Rita, as well as all of her savings. There is also insurance money, and there are a few other sources of income. But for everyone involved, this is uncharted territory.

What's laid on the table between Bill and Rita is unknown to the rest of us, but I do know that someone, be it Bill or Susan (Rita's financial advisor), has to gain control. There isn't a large amount of money, but there is a bulk sum that lands in her lap due to Mozie's death, and there are small amounts dribbling in. Left to herself, Rita will spend it. All of it

Rita wants to sell the house and buy another house in the country; she wants a barn and animals. In reality she can't even change the sheets on her bed, much less run a household with acreage.

Bill pursues his plan and Rita balks. He lays out a financial spreadsheet for her to see, and this develops into a very messy albeit unavoidable situation. I've known Bill since I was fourteen and he has always been fair, soft spoken and honest. Bill loves his sister and he realizes that unless her spending is kept under control, she'll be living under a tree near the Willamette River. Bill wants Rita on a budget and he suggests to Rita that she will be unable to withdraw money every time she has an idea or a whim.

Rita seeks legal counsel, perhaps with the help of Susan, and finds a place that offers free legal services. The end result is obvious; Rita and Bill have to go to court to work this out. The siblings both dig in and won't budge.

On the other side of the fence are her friends who receive daily phone calls about her brother. Rita calls not only me and Murray, but she calls Marta (the banker), Andy and Dennis for advice and to vent. She rants and makes false accusations about her brother. She accuses him of planning to steal her money and inheritance. She yells into the receiver, "It is my money, my house, not Bill's!" We know Bill doesn't want the house or her money. He just wants to block Rita from selling the home and making drastic financial mistakes.

In her phone calls for the next year or more, Rita hates Bill. She claims he is overpowering her and wants to put her in a care home. Plus she hates everyone involved that dares to be on Bill's side. Of course we know there are no sides, so we listen—and pray a tree will fall on our houses and knock out the phone lines. All the while, we are secretly behind Bill. He has no intention of stealing her money or placing her in a home. Sometimes when she phones I want to stick a needle in my eye. Rita goes on and on with the exact same story she's told me the day before, and the day before that. She calls her brother the same names and she tells me her next move, which is the same idea she's had from the beginning: court. Rita does not want a guardian.

This particular section of her life is very difficult; she is so negative and hostile. It appears Rita's issues are more than just Bill, who unfortunately has become the scapegoat. The years of frustration have come to a head and this explodes to the level of venom. Poor brother Bill is the brunt of her anger, her sadness over Mozie's death, and her sexual frustration. Although she thinks she clearly understands what he is trying to do (steal her money), she seriously has no idea what his intentions actually are.

We friends have to listen and be patient. With each of her phone calls, I dare not skip out with an excuse for hanging up, as she is much too distraught. It's all about us listening. We are on the receiving end of very dark negative nightly phone calls. Oh dear. I can't speak for the rest of us, but I learn how to do many chores with a phone between my shoulder and ear. I confess that I tune her out sometimes. If there is a lull in her one sided conversation, I say, "Hmmm," or "Ok," and she continues.

To me it seems more like a three year battle, but Murray is sure it lasts one year only. It is a year of Rita spitting venom at her brother.

This must be a very difficult time for Bill, who is only trying to help. He tries to explain, and tries to make her understand. Through it all, Bill is an amazing human being; he keeps his cool and does what he has to do. There is no way he is going to walk away and give Rita total control over the money. Not once does he outwardly show any signs of anger towards his sister.

One day Rita turns again to Susan for legal advice, but Susan sides with Bill, trying to explain finances to Rita. She listens and stews about it, then fires Susan, or as Murray puts it, "Rita gives Susan the axe." Rita has always been well known for flashing dirty looks, but what used to be funny isn't any more. Now she means it.

On one of our trips north to visit Rita in Eugene, I ask her if she still has the *Rubber Soul* album by the Beatles that I'd loaned her. She says she has it, no problem. "It's in a stack with your dad's photo and some other letters you've sent me." I ask her where she keeps her files and she quickly responds, in all seriousness, "They're in the oven."

I can't keep my cool and yell, "Did you just say, the oven?"

She matter-of-factly replies, "Yes. I never cook, so it's the perfect place."

She walks into the kitchen with me hot on her trail. She bends over, opens the oven door as if to pull out a tin of cupcakes, and hands me my Rubber Soul album and some papers her mother had put in a manila envelope marked "Banana." I take the stack of paperwork and sit at the dining room table with my mouth open. I thumb through the papers and take what I'd loaned her. I hold up my album perpendicular to see if it's warped from being inside the warm filing cabinet, but no. It's flat as a pancake. Out of curiosity, I go back into the kitchen to peek inside the oven. I'll be damned; it is her filing cabinet, and it's an oven full of papers. Someone along the lineup of friends and helpers has the foresight to turn off the pilot light, so I guess the oven is indeed a good place for her papers, and handy too. Rita can make toast and coffee, then open the oven to peruse her files. It's as odd has heck, no doubt about it, but Rita dear has her own operation going on.

More phone calls and seemingly endless Bill bashing. I work around the house, thumb through a magazine or step out onto my patio as she raves on about her stealing cheating brother, and adds, "If only Mozie were still here!"

Murray, on the other hand, decides to be straight with Rita. She explains to Rita that Bill loves her and he always has. "He is family Rita. Your sister-in-law Genia, your niece and nephew—they all love you Rita, and they only want the best for you. You are alienating your family, Rita, and you need to swallow your pride and pain and reconnect with them. Bill is an architect; he doesn't want your money, he never has. And he doesn't want your home either. He is looking out for your best interests and he's trying to help you stay safe." Finally, Murray concludes, "You'll spend more money fighting Bill than if you just trust him and let him help you."

I don't know whether Murray gets through to Rita or if she's just finally had enough. But one day they come to an agreement, and the delicate issue is settled out of court just as suddenly as it began.

All of Rita's needs are met. Her money is in the bank and she has to have a co-signer (I'm sure) to withdraw it. She never likes restraints and boundaries; this is how she was raised. But life without Mozie gives Rita new perspective, and she needs to accept this and move forward.

When I interviewed Bill for this book, he told me that he invested Rita's money in the stock market and during this time the market was on its way up. Rita did very well. I have a suspicion he never told Rita she doubled her money. If he had, I'm sure she'd have been on the next plane to Las Vegas.

With her hatred for Bill quelled, Rita now sets her sights on her mother's doctor. She wants to sue the doctor who she feels intentionally killed her mother. For a year, Rita repeatedly drives to the doctor's office and waits in the parking lot until he walks out to his car. She gets out of her truck and begins to scream. She accuses him of being a murderer and of not doing enough to keep her mother alive. This is typical of a person with a head injury. They magnify problems and just can't let go. In Rita's mind, Marie's doctor must have killed her, or at least let her die, because Mozie would never have left Rita otherwise. The same type of logic drove Rita's attacks on Bill and Susan.

Life continues to move forward for our friend. She and Bill have made peace, Rita has agreed to the money terms, and she hesitantly begins to understand that her brother is standing tall to help; he is not the enemy. But she never forgives Marie's doctor.

In his defense, I feel I should explain that Marie, out of love for her daughter, keeps her illness to herself. She never lets on to Rita how gravely ill she has become. When Marie goes to the hospital and passes away within the week, Rita is utterly shocked and unprepared. She has no context for what has happened, so her automatic response is to accuse the doctor of not doing more to save her Mozie. Marie conceals her illness with good intentions, but it backfires and pulls the rug out from under Rita. I'm sure if Marie had the benefit of the hindsight I have, she would have been preparing Rita all along.

Friendship isn't about whom you know the longest,
it's about who came and never left your side.

Flying Solo

When the dust settles and the legal battle between brother and sister is over, Rita's life resumes. We brace ourselves as Rita prepares to show the world she can live alone. With the aid of a caregiver, Ruth Ann, life continues as if the court battles and legal papers flying back and forth never happened.

My phone still rings in my ear, especially during a deep sleep. Her question, still spoken with the exact same wording as all the other midnight calls through the years, comes through loud and clear. I answer her question about her virginity status as I have before: "Yes, you are a virgin." I do confess to changing up my answer once, long ago. I thought she wanted to hear, "No Rita, you are not a virgin," but this answer played havoc in her mind. Somewhere deep down inside she knows the truth; she knows the answer but needs continual confirmation. Of course there is no way to prove this. A physical exam is certainly out of question.

Marie had become a super mom after the accident, and had kept a close eye on her daughter. Her mother's intuition and alertness was never over-obvious, but Mozie knew the score. She carefully observed and never over shadowed her daughter, and never gave Rita the feeling she was being watched or smothered. Nevertheless it was Marie who brought home the groceries, prepared all the meals, and suggested to Rita when it was time to shower. Marie often gave her a gentle nudge to clean the bathroom, or sweep the patio. True, Rita's balance was sacrificed in the car accident, and her knees were never again as functional as they should be. The surgeries and physical therapy didn't seem to give her all the momentum, strength or flexibility she needed. Still, Marie kept at her to move about, sweep, mow the lawn and play with her cats.

Now, with Mozie gone, Rita flounders. First, she is alone and she goes toe to toe with her brother, Bill. Next she blows a cork and fires Susan, her legal and financial assistant. Finally, she stalks and verbally attacks Marie's poor doctor.

It is apparent that Rita is slipping into a depression, and it's no surprise she has suppressed anger issues from the sad turn her life has taken. No one can grab her hand and pull her back. She begins to spend more time at the *all you can eat* buffet. The more weight she adds, the more impact and stress this has on her knees. She begins to spiral downward.

Dennis informs me that Rita called him one evening to tell him about her ordeal at a movie theater. She went to the movies alone, and after the two hour movie was over, she was unable to stand. Instead of asking for help, Rita told Dennis, she began to crawl down the carpeted aisle of the movie theater toward the lobby, and she continued to crawl outside to the parking lot towards her truck. She told Dennis that a few people offered to help, but Rita preferred to crawl and struggle along on her hands and knees. I can just imagine her telling her would-be helpers, "No, thank you, I'm fine," as she crawls over a tar-covered parking lot.

One night Rita phones Murray, and maybe Marta too, about the water incident. She doesn't phone me, as she knows I've hit some difficult emotional times. And anyway, she's calling in her role as homeowner; she often focuses on Murray and Marta for help with maintenance problems.

Rita tells them her bedroom floor is wet, with about an inch of water, and her feet are wet too. Murray asks her, "How much water Rita, is it just in your bedroom, or is the water throughout your house?" Rita relates that the water is all over the house. She tells Murray that her cats are ok; they're watching from the back of the couch. Murray, in a panic tells Rita to phone a plumber, El Pronto! She explains to Rita about broken pipes and leaks, and warns her that the water will continue to rise. Murray orders Rita, "Hang up the phone now, and call a plumber."

Rita casually says, "Ok, I will," and they click off.

The following day, close to noon (this is early morning to Rita), Murray gets another call. Rita describes to Murray that when she woke up, she sat up on the edge of her bed and reached for her slippers, but felt water instead. When she stood up, the water was up to her calves, and her slippers were floating next to her bed. Murray goes bonkers.

As Murray relates this story to me over the phone, I'm speechless, and swallow hard. Mulling this over, I take a deep breath and suggest we either phone Bill or Rita's care worker Ruth Ann. We both feel helpless living so far away.

I imagine her slippers floating aimlessly in her bedroom, her cats' soggy litter box with cat turds floating about, stacks of newspapers on the floor in a soggy mess. Oh dear, this can't be happening. No one asks Rita why she chose to go to bed instead of phoning a plumber. It's Rita's way of dealing with an issue. In Rita's experience, all problems go away by morning. And since she has trouble with her short term memory, that's usually true. But it doesn't apply to broken pipes. I pretend to phone her out of the blue and happily ask how life is going these days. Oh boy do I get an ear full. She says her life is worse than a bad B movie, except it's real. This phone call lasts for two hours, and all I can do is listen.

When Murray calls back, she resorts to spitting out some old familiar high school cuss words. She tells Rita to get on the phone and call a damn plumber, right now! She has to explain to her again that a leak will not go away; it must be dealt with. She lectures Rita about all the possible damage, then yells, "Phone an f***ing plumber, Rita! Do it right now! Call someone in Eugene—a friend, a helper, or someone you work with at the clinic. Get on it, Rita. You cannot wait."

Rita calmly tells Murray with a giggle that she caught her floating slippers, and put them on. Laughing, she describes how she sloshed into the kitchen to get a Bear Claw for breakfast and ate it standing at the kitchen counter with water around her lower legs. She further describes that the cat box is full of wet litter (just as I'd envisioned), and her cats are still lying on the back of the couch witnessing the whole fiasco. At this, she laughs even louder. To Rita, this is a joke, not a problem.

Rita walks through the pond to the dining room and opens the sliding glass door, which lets out some of the water. Then she wades to the front door and does the same. Seriously, I think she is enjoying the change of pace.

Rita finally phones a plumber, and yes it is a broken pipe. Her choice to sleep instead of phone for help costs Rita many, many thousands of dollars. Her home owner's insurance kicks in and picks up some of the tab. The insurance adjuster comes out to assess the damage and he phones a contractor. The contractor gives a bid, and extensive work begins throughout the interior of her home.

He replaces all of her doors, her kitchen and bathroom cabinets, the closet doors, baseboards, and wood flooring. She has to replace her couch and she loses several cardboard boxes full of her mother's books and collectibles. There are many other items that are soaked or have damage. She and Ruth Ann sort, clean and lay out keepsakes and junk all mixed together. They put everything in the garage to dry, all in an organized row. Ruth Ann spends many days and weeks helping Rita sort through and save her things. They organize, salvage what keepsakes they can, and clean.

I suppose Rita stays in a motel and her cats are placed at the Humane Society until they are able to move back home. Murray shakes her head and reiterates, "Rita just went to bed! She went to sleep knowing there was a pipe leaking water all over her house! What's next Banana?"

Rita now sleeps twelve to eighteen hours a day. Her steady weight gain contributes to her fatigue and depression. She misses her mother terribly and she tires of making decisions. Rita is also lonely, very lonely.

We friends have full lives and can't drive up as often as we used to. We work full-time and some have medical problems—back, knees, you name it. Life is more complex as we grow older. I lose Jeff during this time and am not mentally able to guide and help my friend.

On a warm spring day, a few months after the water invasion, Rita phones Murray in a panic. She describes a horrifying yet comical scene. She's in her fenced back yard, standing on the grass playing with her cats with a string, when whoosh! A feral cat darts out of the shrubs and runs inside her open sliding glass door. Rita rushes into her house to shoo away the unwelcomed cat, but she is no match for this trained survivor. She lets her own cats back inside to give it a try, but they just run and hide under her bed. Rita does everything she can to remove the obnoxious intruder. The cat instantly begins to back up and spray her furniture and everything else. It leaves a calling card throughout her newly refurbished interior. The cat sprays the new kitchen cabinets, her bedspread, and every door, while Rita continues to yell "Yaaaaaah" and hit the bed and walls with her cane.

The feral cat eats most of her cats' food, so Rita buys more. She doesn't think to wipe the furniture, she just chases the cat round and round in circles. Her renovations are only months old; her home was as fresh as a daisy. Now, it gets a nice little *spray* to seal the deal.

Rita's new unwelcomed feline is still being fed. This feral cat doesn't stay overnight or a day or two, he runs around inside her home with Rita chasing him for three months. Murray calls me about this situation and says she suspects Rita likes chasing the cat, that it's a welcome game and causes her to laugh.

One day Rita hears a knock at her front door. She opens the door and there are two women—one young and one older—who ask if they can share a message with her. She invites the Jehovah's Witnesses to come inside. According to Dennis, who heard it straight from Rita, they step inside, take one whiff, then step back outside, hand her a Watch Tower, and take off. Although they're polite, they quickly retreat from her front porch. It's pretty clear that the overwhelming stench of cat spray is the reason these two lovely people run away.

Finally, Rita calls Murray and tells her that this morning, she opened the sliding glass door to step outside, and the feral cat whipped past her and jumped back over the fence. This cat finally realized that life is better down by the creek. Good riddance! Murray thinks. But the damage is done. Ruth Ann comes by with cleaning supplies and they start all over again.

Between the cat spray and Rita not remembering to take showers, her house is very fragrant. Murray is feeling physically better after a mishap she had while painting a house. She decides to drive up alone and check out the situation. She steps inside the living room and tells Rita that her house reeks of cat shit, filth and BO.

Rita says, "Really?" and Murray replies, "Yes, Chickie, your house smells bad; now let's get out of here." Murray can't stay long, and they've planned to go out for lunch. But she's in the house long enough to get an eye full and a nose full of a very serious problem.

Murray finds the phone number for the Merry Maids Service and advises Rita to get her house cleaned right away. She has a caregiver, but what she really needs is a personal hygiene keeper and a supervisor, preferably one with a whip. Before she leaves, Murray strongly suggests Rita take a shower.

When she gets back home, Murray phones and tells me that Rita's house is in need of all new furniture and bedding. We discuss how Rita probably views things: she has a roof over her head, she has well-behaved and much loved cats, and she has well-organized kindling and fire wood. "I guess that's all a girl needs," Murray concludes.

The following year I take a weekend trip with a friend to Portland to attend a car show. On our way home we stop in Eugene. Rita waits for our visit. My friend is towing his Cobra, and we know Rita will love to see this classic sports car. It's been a while, and now she and I can finally visit.

We arrange to meet at a pizza parlor. But when we get there, instead of the happy encounter and conversation we're expecting, Rita is extremely agitated. She skips her usual questions about my two children, and instead asks if I remember the beautiful silver spruce that Mozie planted in their yard the day they moved in. I do remember it. It's the one Murray chased Dana around when she was just two years old, running, giggling and squealing as they played. The tree has grown in height and beauty and is truly lovely, sitting as it does in the center of the front lawn on the corner lot of a shady street. Rita is fuming.

Earlier that day, Rita tells us, there was a knock on her front door. It was her neighbor, asking if Rita had looked outside lately. She stepped out to look, and someone had taken a hatchet to that tree, and cut the whole thing down. Rita is angry and hurt and sad and furious. She cusses and pounds the table with her fist. She takes angry bites of pizza, long sips of soda, and continues to rant about her tree. We listen and eat. She doesn't cope with this type of invasion, and she can't control her emotions very well. We can't blame her. No one would be cool after such a senseless massacre. But with head injuries, frustration is ten times worse; the invasion and injustice magnify. We are quiet, and my friend John offers to buy another pine tree, dig a hole and plant it. Rita can't deal with a solution at this point. She has to get past the anger to even consider a replacement tree.

Finally, we are suffering from pizza overload and give our boxed up pizza to Rita. We walk outside and she stops when she sees John's trailer towing the Cobra. She walks over to it with us, touches the car, and begins to ask a lot of questions. She wants to know, "How fast does it go? Does it sound real loud when you turn on the engine? How much does one of these cost? Where did you get it?" She touches the paint job, the tires, and she is lost in a moment of love for fast cars, forgetting about the pine tree.

Later she drives back to her house with the stub of a tree on the front lawn. It is very sad and very wrong. Who would do this to Rita? I wonder. Later in the week she finds out it is a punk teenager down the street. Rita never has trusted this kid, and suspects he's the one even before he walks with his father to her house and apologizes. Rita tells him it's too late for apologies. "This particular tree can never be replaced," she explains.

When I hear about him coming over and confessing his crime, it's a feeling of watching my friend go down in flames. She suffers extreme highs and extreme lows. This keepsake—a living tree-cut down and killed, well, it's the worst case scenario. Rita begins to sleep all the time, and doesn't care much about her kindling or helping at the clinic. She used to help out now and then, but now just getting the gumption to get up and go is a huge chore. I'm at a loss and have no idea how to help, so I mail her some t-shirts and pictures of my kids.

Back home I have fantasies of showing up at her house with rubber gloves and bleach spray and a mask. I dream of doing all of her laundry, painting her living room, buying her a computer and teaching her how to look things up on the internet. This would definitely cross her boundaries and probably make her resent me; then I'd be the evil one. So I just dream of it and continue to talk to her on the phone. Our calls grow more frequent, and always late at night—often in the middle of the night. Her phone conversations with me, Murray and a few others help keep Rita afloat.

Life for Rita is serious and her frustrations mount. Then one day a very small scale joy begins to sprout. A woman named Sue, who's a counselor at the clinic for the disabled, asks Rita to be a volunteer. Though Rita qualifies to get treatment there herself, she finds she is very capable of helping people, and ends up spending most of her time helping the blind. She reads to them and guides them whenever needed. This part of her life is very rewarding and she regains her self-worth. Her daily trips to the clinic help her go on living without her Mozie. She looks forward to spending time at the center, and loves to help.

She soon realizes that she is better off than most of the other people being served at the clinic. This revelation gives her hope, lifts her spirits, and raises her self-esteem. Rita is now one of the regular volunteers in the care group for the blind. She loves helping, and she loves the counselors too.

One day the counselors plan a weekend getaway for the blind clients and their helpers. They rent an extra-large beach house. The plan is to caravan from Eugene due west to a town called Florence, which is located on the coast. They loan Rita a car to drive and she is put in charge of transporting three blind companions. The weather is sunny and bright, and everyone's in great spirits. Rita is very happy; she loves to help and loves to drive. Plus, someone else is paying for the gas—it's a win-win.

Rita's car is the last one in the caravan. They drive along through a small tourist town and she stops for a yellow light. The other cars continue to drive. One of her passengers asks Rita if she can stop somewhere to pick up bottles of water and snacks. So when the light changes Rita turns left and drives into a Safeway parking lot. The three women get out and Rita walks with them slowly, leading them into the store. Rita helps to locate the bottled water section and then finds the snack section. She makes sure they stay together, then leads them to the checkout stand and helps each person pay.

They walk outside into the open air and stand there. Rita makes sure they stay together in a group, but still they stand. "Why aren't we moving?" one of the women asks. She doesn't want to say so, but Rita has forgotten where she parked. It's not her truck, it's a loaner car, and she can't remember what kind of car she's driving or what color it is. Hoping they will remember which direction they went after she parked and stepped out of the car, Rita takes the group for a walk-about. Through the parking lot they go, but no one can remember exactly which direction they went to get to the store. Rita refuses to ask the store manager for help because she is afraid she'll get in trouble and lose her position. Then Rita sees a bench and decides that sitting down is a good idea.

Meanwhile, the other cars in the caravan pull over to the side of the road to stretch and assess how much longer the trip will take. They wait for Rita to pull up behind them. They wait, and she is nowhere in sight. The head counselor tells the others, "Wait here; I'm going to look for Rita." She gets back into her car, flips a U-turn and begins to back track in search of Rita and her passengers. She searches for the car, looking up and down side streets, and then notices the Safeway store. She drives right past Rita and the blind trio on their bench, but Rita doesn't notice her because by this time they have taken out their snacks and are munching and visiting. The counselor sees Rita's loaner car in the lot and parks nearby to investigate. She walks through the parking lot searching for the four of them before going inside to check there. Then she spots a group sitting serenely on the city bus bench. She walks closer to the benchwarmers, and sure enough there's dear Rita with her new friends, sitting under a large plastic arch. They're eating, talking, laughing—and waiting to be rescued.

When Rita sees her rescuer, she says in her sultry voice, "Well, it's about time," and they all laugh and slap their legs. With the counselor's help, Rita leads the students back to the borrowed car, and this time the counselor makes sure Rita follows closely behind. This adventure has a positive ending.

Rita still and forever will grieve the absence of her mother. But she does her best to stay busy and be helpful to others. She also proves she is capable of living on her own, even if she has more mishaps than most.

> I am so glad you let me get the piano for you.
> It is actually a large thank you.
> I admire and appreciate all the things you do
> It is because of you that I enjoy living. Without you I would only be existing

> BE SLOW TO FALL INTO FRIENDSHIP;
> BUT WHEN THOU ART IN,
> CONTINUE FIRM AND CONSTANT.
>
> *Socrates*

New Crush

YEARS AND YEARS PASS BY, and Rita's phone calls grow further apart. The topics we discuss are mostly about her driving excursions and the help she gives at different clinics. Still, without fail, she asks me how the kids are doing. The tables turn and I begin to phone her, because the repetitive phone calls that once were a nuisance have now become addictive, and I long for our chats and banter.

Rita phones one summer night in early June. She starts off with the exact same wording of the all too familiar sentence which I've listened to for decades: "Hi Banana, I hope I'm not calling at a bad time, but I was wondering if you know whether or not I'm a lesbian." A lesbian? Did I miss something? I wonder why she has a change of heart concerning the male species. I take a deep breath, and think, Oh, no! Not this again. Another thirty years of questions.

I gather my thoughts, run to the living room, curl up on the couch in my robe, and flatly and emphatically reply, "No Rita, you are not a lesbian; you've always liked men."

Without hesitation she continues on her love story. She hasn't heard a word I said. She tells me, "I enrolled in a class to help me understand and cope with my head injury. The teacher, Sue, is tall, and has a very pleasant face, and is really nice and she is smart too, and I have a huge crush on her." Just like her repetitive calls about her virginity, these phone calls continue multiple times a week. But this time Rita is more aggressive; she not only thinks about it, and she not only calls me and Murray to talk about it, but this time she also approaches Sue, who fortunately is a Social Worker and is trained to handle these types of situations. Rita tells me she has confessed to Sue that she likes her lot, and asks her if she wants to go out to the movies sometime. Sue handles Rita with great professional care. She politely turns down her offer, but Rita continues to be smitten.

In the coming month I have time to think about what I've said to my dear friend. I seriously think about Rita and about my answer. I'm armed and ready when the next midnight call comes in, and this is my new speech: "Rita, I'm in no position to say whether or not you're a lesbian." She listens quietly, and I continue, "You have asked me a very personal question, and I have to tell you today, Rita—now listen to me—no one knows another person's mind or what's in their heart. I have no idea what you're thinking or feeling, I really don't, Rita. This is important, now listen. I need to tell you to be yourself. Find someone you feel happy with, be it a man or a woman, and be happy."

She says, "Thank you for saying that to me, Banana," as if I have just given her permission to be a chick stalker. But in reality, I'm telling her this: no one else can answer her personal choices in life. No one can choose her love or mate, no one but her.

Rita is enthralled with Sue because she helps her; she is kind and she gets Rita involved in projects and asks her to help with others not so fortunate. Sue sees something in Rita; she sees potential and she watches her interact and sees her compassion toward those less fortunate than herself. I think it's interesting that Rita ends up doing the same type of work she started doing in her dream job in Fresno, just before her accident.

Rita decides she wants to be in charge of mowing the lawns at the clinic where she gets help (and helps). I'm sure her desire to be on a riding lawnmower has something to do with her love of sports cars, and this is the closest and safest thing she can get. But the clinic, it seems, has rules. They believe it is a hazard to have one of the patients on a riding lawn mower, and sadly they say no. I have to say that this decision was a mistake. Rita, being a perfectionist, would have mowed those lawns to look like the fanciest landscaping in the area.

Eventually Rita does give a piece of herself to the facility she is so heavily involved in helping. She donates her treasured piano. I'm sure her fondness for Sue is a factor, but Rita genuinely loves the clinic and knows they saved her life by trusting her and giving her a reason to continue on. She writes a wonderful note: "No need to thank me. It is me that needs to thank you." The piano is still there today turning out wonderful music. It's played frequently with passion, although I'll bet the player doesn't hit all of the keys with the palms of their hands and yell, "No more!" at the end of each piece like Rita used to do.

Rita continues to phone us. Murray still talks to her for many hours at a time, and we are her sounding board for more years to come. Murray has a soothing effect on Rita, and she talks to her with a calmness I lack. Murray uses great care and kindness and patience when speaking to Rita, but

still Murray has to tell Rita point blank about her situation: "If you're interested in meeting a woman, you'd better take a shower Chickie. You've already scared off a feral cat." This makes Rita laugh out loud, and then she sighs because Murray is right. Rita is a handful, a bag of mixed emotions and questions accompanied by health and breathing issues. Her weight gain causes her great distress in breathing and walking. Rita now walks with the use of two canes; her balance has never been fully conquered, so she avoids uneven ground. She still speaks a with a slight slur, and her eyes-those beautiful eyes-still have a slight vacant look. But now her eyes hold a worried expression, too. They tell her story; one can see in her eyes the expression of someone who has endured great suffering of body and heart.

Her new crush shows us a clear example of Rita's desire to be loved, noticed and appreciated. It also shows how much she misses her little Mozie. Eventually Rita begins to ease back on her idea of dating someone who has continually rejected her. She begins to accept her fate of never having true romance. I wasn't all that surprised when I heard about her epiphany-her love for Sue. I just could not contemplate her ever releasing herself to another.

At one point, Marie had decided it was time for "The Kid" to have a check-up, and she took Rita to a gynecologist. The nurse showed Rita where to put her feet in the stirrups, and the doctor stepped between her legs and began the exam; Rita flipped out and went totally ballistic. She fought her mother, the nurse and the doctor. She tore off her paper dress and dove for her clothes. They finally gave up and suggested she calmly get dressed behind the curtain, and she could rebook her appointment for a better time. That time never arrived. Rita had no intention of letting anyone near her gommie, not that day or ever.

One afternoon in early February the phone rings and I happen to be home—it must be a Sunday. Rita is having lots of breathing problems from her pre-existing injuries, her previously punctured lungs. I answer, "Hello," and on the other end of the line is a medley of coughing; I sit on the rescued oak stool from the Porterville City Library and listen to hacking, choking and more coughing. I wait until she tries to speak, there's a pause, then a few more coughs. Hearing an opening, a breath and then silence, I take my cue and blurt out, "Hey, Rita, what have you been doing lately?"

She yells back, "Coughing!"

Her quick response catches me off guard; I don't expect this answer and my reaction is a howl of laughter. "Whew, that was funny, Rita, and quick too." Though she sounds croupy, she too begins to laugh, but her chuckle is mixed with a rumbling cough. She says she'll call me back later when we can talk. I cheerfully ask her, "Are you ok?"

She coughs and chugs out, "Do I sound ok?"

And so it goes; she is still in there—that acerbic quick wit, the sexual frustration, and her sweet vulnerability.

Three days later she phones again. I sit on the edge of my bed, looking into my backyard and I listen. Rita is sixty-one now. In just twelve days she'll be turning 62, so I rib her a little bit since she's two years older than I am. "Well, you sound much better today Pita girl." She laughs and says coughing is the pits.

This call is different from all the others. She doesn't talk about her nonexistent love life, or about her life at all. She avoids the topic of seminars and her *would-be* sexual prey. She only asks about my two surviving children and she wants to know what they're doing. She listens as I proudly tell her about their lives and accomplishments, marriages and kids. She again tells me she is sorry about Jeff, though he's been gone nearly twenty years. "He was a cool kid, and I liked him a lot." It was a very nice conversation between two old friends. Then she says the most amazing thing. She says, "Thank you for having patience with me all these years, and thanks for being a good friend." But I really wasn't that patient, deep down inside.

Her flattering statement makes me giggle from guilt so I quickly respond with, "You're welcome, Rita. It's what friends do."

She coughs a little and sounds like she's getting a little bit croupy, then says, "Nice talking to you, Banana." She needs to go; I can hear it in her voice. We sweetly say goodbye, knowing we'll talk again soon.

Two days later Dennis calls. Again I happen to be in the back bedroom, and I sit down on the edge of the bed next to the end table-the exact same spot where I sat when Rita called. Dennis softly says, "Rita died today."

The phone tumbles out of my hands.

A FRIEND IS SOMEONE WHO UNDERSTANDS YOUR PAST,
BELIEVES IN YOUR FUTURE AND ACCEPTS YOU
JUST THE WAY YOU ARE.

Tijuana Rose

MURRAY AND I DON'T TALK to each other for a couple of years, nor do I talk to any of our other friends—except Dennis—just him. After Rita's passing, Murray and I are both talked out. There's nothing left to say, so we each back off and live our lives. Finally, after three years we decide to meet at Dennis' house in our hometown, and invite friends to join us with lots of food and drink to honor and have a memorial for Rita. Some of us bring photos to share, a scrap book, stories. The stories roll out all evening. I set up a framed 8 by 10 photo of Rita, taken one year before her accident; Dennis places this on the side table.

Laughing, I finally ask Dennis how Rita got the nick name *Tijuana Rose*. He tells this story: Rita hadn't been around town like she usually was; no one had seen her over the weekend. So Dennis phoned her and woke her up. He point blank asked her what she'd been doing lately and he wasn't prepared for her explanation. She'd met a Mexican guy at Coleman's who told her his woes. He was trying to get back home, across the border. Rita told Dennis she felt sorry for this guy so she gave him a ride to Tijuana, Mexico. Dennis the unshakable was speechless with her answer. He was also surprised with her lack of common sense towards danger, even though she told him the guy was very nice and he appreciated the ride.

This story leads Dennis to tag Rita with her lifelong nickname, Tijuana Rose. I've read many letters Rita sent to Dennis while he was away at college, and these letters are signed, "Tijuana Rose," or "Hot Sauce, and keep it that way," and on one envelope she scribbled, "CC Rider, or TJ Rose." Sometimes she'd leave a note and sign it "TJ."

Andy meets up with us at the memorial also. She and I haven't seen each other for forty-eight years; we hug and look at each other's faces, our adult grandma faces. The elusive Murray shows up, and so do many other friends. Rita's memorial turns into a Roach Avenue School invasion. Burger is there even though she didn't attend Roach (thank goodness, I have someone on my side), and Marta too. Susan Boyer, a lifelong friend of Rita's and part of the Roach Gang, shows up too. We talk about Rita and laugh loud over her pranks and quick one-liners. We discover that some of her dirty looks are captured on film. We talk about how Rita loved to look evil, scary, harsh and sly. And we discuss how unusual her life was, too. Her grandmother GaGa and her suave mother Marie lived life as if they were on a daily TV show. We all remember that Rita's home was different from other homes, different in a good stimulating way, with freedom to think out of the box.

Murray relates to us that when she and Rita were just kids they used to ask GaGa to drive them downtown at 2:00 A.M. Rita told her where to park, then they would get out of the car run down the block to some vending machines and steal cokes. GaGa sat in her car waiting and had no idea what these two darling girls were up to or why they needed to go downtown. But she was always happy to drive them downtown and back home whenever they asked.

We laugh until our stomachs hurt. We pass around the scrap book and each one of us has a story to share. The room is full of friends and we blow life back into Rita.

Andy cooks some great hot dishes for us, because at our age we need to eat and refuel. Burger brings food and Dennis supplies us with snacks also. Andy and Murray offer wine from their bottles on the kitchen counter. It's a feast with old friends. We scoot in close around Dennis's huge round antique table, we eat and reminisce about our much loved and missed friend. Rita finally receives her long overdue and fond farewell from her hometown gang. Burger keeps slapping her leg and saying, "God love her," then she wails with laughter. Marta adds her carefully spoken words about the person she's loved since they were very young girls. Marta's a no nonsense woman with a very poignant delivery. To listen when Marta tells a story about their pranks is to tag along. She's a great story teller.

Murray, as cool as ever, sits back, smiles and listens and sometimes adds her shocking two cents. Dennis smiles and chuckles all night but not once does he mention a word about his early teenage drinking binges with Rita. He specifically omits the pink macaroni he left all over town and on the side of Norman's caddy.

Murray begins to laugh and tells us about her and Rita hiding in the hall closet. Every week they hid together, as quiet as two mice, and waited for GaGa to come home from her weekly Bridge club. They heard her shoes as she walked through the back door and through the kitchen, and she always took a short cut through the den, which is Marie's bedroom. She continued down the hall, clomp, clomp, and clomp. She'd be halfway to her bedroom when, wham! The girls would open the door, jump out and scream as loud and mean as possible "GaGa!" She always and forever grabbed her heart and gasped, "You scared me!" But, as Murray laughingly explains, "this went on every single week, the same evening, at about the same time." Murray says that she and Rita decide GaGa's in on the game. We laugh so much because Andy then adds how she was also a witness many times to this torment. Andy sat on the couch and watched Rita as she hid in the closet waiting for GaGa to walk by. As soon as she did, wham! "GaGa!"

I chime in and tell the group a story I've never told my kids. When I first met Rita, she taught me how to hot wire a phone in a phone booth. We squeezed into a phone booth, she showed me how to split the wires, hot wire the phone, and listen to the dial tone. Then she told me I could call anywhere long distance, and for free. I didn't know anyone's phone number out of town, so I'd call my Grandma around the corner on H Street.

Miss Rita, we hope you are listening. You taught us the words *scuzzie*, and *five dolla'* and you explained about the red light district. You told us what a hooker was and what a pimp was. You taught me how to light a fire cracker, and showed me the two different ways to flip the bird. "This is the angry bird and this is a social bird," you explained. You taught most of us how to roll up a sleeping bag nice and tight, how to light a camp fire, and how to check oil using a dip stick. Rita, you also trusted me with scissors and a razor before I knew what I was doing.

It is because of Rita, Murray and Dennis that I have to rip three pages out of my yearbook to hide their raunchy comments and pictures. Life threw Rita a curve ball and she survived. Her multiple broken bones eventually healed, and she regained her speech. Learning the names of things we take for granted every day was a victory for her. She also learned how drive, passed her test and got her license. She eventually learned how to survive on her own, not well, but at least she tried. She fought a good long battle and she died on her own terms.

Rita never mentioned she was in an assisted living complex, even for the short two months she lived there. I've always wondered why she didn't share this with me, and I wonder if she was frightened. She never shared with me the fact she was under strict medical orders not to eat dairy products. Taking orders and following directions were never her strong points. Rita only listened to one person and that was her independent stubborn inner child. Naturally when she was craving her favorite drink and was told no, she ordered it from the kitchen—a root beer float. She'd charge it to her room and enjoy something wonderful and satisfying.

I'd like to imagine she closed her eyes and passed away to greener pastures with a smirk on her face. My heart wants to believe this, but in reality, COPD (Chronic Obstructive Pulmonary Disease) is a very painful lung/heart disease, and I hope she was well taken care of in her last hours. She left this earth on a Thursday morning, before sunrise, in February, her birthday month. Ten days shy of turning 62.

For you, the reader, her full name is Rita Marie Simpson. In *Book One* I recall her wild and crazy life before her accident; what a fun ride this was. To be her friend you had to be ready for anything, anytime and be ready to go for long rides with no destination. If you can't hang onto a coat tail in a tornado then you wouldn't have lasted as her friend.

Book Two flows into Rita's second life. She lived a long frustrating journey of confusion, yearning, relearning, sexual fantasies, and questions concerning her virginity. Sometimes she'd experience a rare and wonderful moment of clarity, then just as quickly, revert back to her struggles. Rita was deeply loved by everyone who came into contact with her, and she left a long trail of friends behind. Her name still comes up in conversation, and is always is accompanied with a good laugh.

Here's hoping you enjoyed your ride with Rita. Murray sums it up best; Rita was one in a bazillion.

Betty Jo, Rita, Tish and Andy

Rita

Norman

Rita

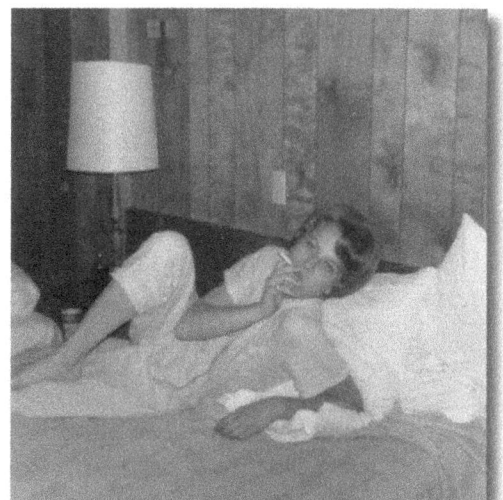
Rita

Jenny and Rita

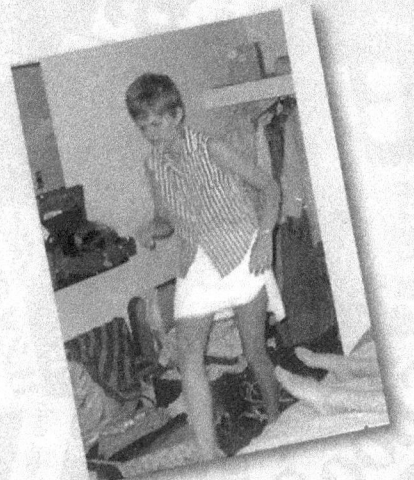
Rita in Reno

Rita and Marie

Rita and Murray

Murray, Banana, and Dennis

THE SIMPLEST QUESTION IN THE MIDDLE OF A
CONVERSATION WILL PRODUCE THE SWEETEST ANSWER.

WHAT DID RITA MEAN TO YOU?

From the Heart

ANDREA FERGUSON SOUZA (ANDY)
Andy was quiet, and then began to tell the story of her friend Rita:

Rita was the first person I met on the first day of Kindergarten. We were only five years old and our birthdays were five days apart. I always felt a kinship to Rita. I respected Rita's mother Marie and her relationship with Rita after they moved to Oregon. Rita and Murray were funny pranksters, and this began at a young age. I traveled to Yellowstone with Rita and her mother, then onto the Seattle World's Fair in 1962. I loved Rita then, and still do.

Rita was held back in seventh grade. I assume this was due to her father's sudden death that resulted in Rita becoming a late bloomer, and she felt her safe place was an immature place. Holding Rita back a year landed her in the same class as Murray and this match became an unstoppable duo.

Judy Murray Schmeichel
Murray thought about this question for a moment while I waited with high anticipation, then she gave the most sweet and simple explanation:

Rita and I thought the same things at the same time, we acted on the same ideas, whether it was a prank or a good laugh, we were always on the same channel. We were on the tennis team together and played at the same level. She was more than a great friend. She always knew what I was thinking and I could always read her thoughts. She was my twin.

Dennis Connor
Dennis sadly remembered his dear friend:

Rita was a free spirit. She was mischievous, generous and she had an amazing quick mind and a salty wit. She was a unique friend and she loved to drive around town or the countryside. I miss her a lot, and always will. When I think about Rita, memories of her always make me smile. It was too bad her life became a struggle.

Marta Boldstad
Marta reflected how Rita was a good friend:

We always, no matter what, had a great time. With her, you always knew there would be much laughing and carrying on. She was never mad at anyone, no matter what happened. She wasn't made that way.

Betty Jo Kyker
Betty Jo's first reaction to this question was laughter.

Rita was absolutely delightful. You just never knew what she'd think up next, and she totally made you laugh. One incident was an idea

From the Heart

Rita concocted: she dressed me up in layers of clothes to resemble a bag lady. And I have no idea where she got all these clothes. Then Rita, Dennis and I drove to Bobbie's house. I knocked on her front door with Rita's instructions. I told Bobbie my name was *Tawnda Laya Wilson*; I used poor grammar, talked like I was on drugs, and told Bobbie I was lost. It was the look of shock, confusion and concern across Bobbie's face that made me crack up. When I started to laugh, Dennis and Rita came out of hiding around the corner from her house. We all had such a great laugh. To this day, I use that name she gave me when I need to come up with a good one.

JUDY WIESENBERGER KUTCHEL (BURGER)
Tenderly, Judy remembers:

I had a blast with Rita, and I loved the lady. We used to ride around in her sports car. Even when it was a cold night, she'd put the top down and we'd drive all over town and about freeze to death, but she didn't seem to mind. Rita was gorgeous and I loved her.

BOBBIE BENTLEY
With sweetness of memory, my sister and I have talked about Rita a thousand times. She said:

Rita was my sister Judi's friend, then she became my friend. I liked her because she was trustworthy. You knew that no matter what you told Rita, or what she witnessed, she would never say a word or betray you. I always enjoyed her and knew she was a friend. Her mother brought Rita by my house a few years after the accident; Rita knocked on the front door, they walked in, and Rita happily said, "Hi Bobbie." Then she said she remembered the grass in my living room. It was my green shag carpet she remembered. Rita had a memory of this carpet and even though she was confused and mixed up her words, she meant green carpet. Her memory was coming back, but it was just a little jumbled in the beginning.

Mickey Sullivan

During this phone interview, Mickey yelled to her husband Larry, "Hey Larry, what did you think of Rita?" and he yelled back, "She was a pain in the ass." We laughed and talked about Rita's crazy sense of humor, and Mickey went on to say:

Life around Rita was always an adventure. Whether we were on a trip or just having a conversation, she was very entertaining and she had her own unique point of view. You could never persuade her to do anything she didn't want to do. Rita used her humor as a shield to keep people away. She always kept a wall up so no one could get in.

Tammy Taylor (Bobbie's daughter)

Tammy recalls Rita through the young eyes of a watchful child in awe:

I still remember Rita coming over to our house after work; she'd be driving her green and black Cougar. She'd get out of the car wearing a pencil skirt, low heels and a cardigan. She would lean against the car and talk to Mom while she smoked. She seemed so sophisticated. I watched her from our bay window; she'd put her head up and blow smoke rings. Then Mom would wave for us to come outside. My brother Roger and I would get into Rita's very nice car with our mom, and she'd take us out for ice cream. She was so cool; I liked to watch her blowing smoke rings.

Ruth Ann Vance
Ruth Ann fondly remembers her charge, Rita:

We became fast friends and shared a million laughs. I think about her every day and will always miss her. She loved the sound of water flowing down a rocky creek bed and she loved the sounds of a train whistle. When I hear these things, I think of my friend.

Judi Loren Grace (Banana)

Rita, my lovely friend; together we crossed the line and thought of each other as sisters. I slept at her house so many times I lost count. We'd lie in her double bed and talk about life, peeping Toms, and I'd tell her beauty secrets I'd read in magazines. These stories—like putting Vaseline on your feet then putting your feet in plastic bags with a rubber band around your ankle—made her bed jiggle as she laughed so hard. Then one night we confessed to each other that we noticed we were beginning to look alike.

Her mother was a very cool mother, but she just didn't realize Rita's maternal needs, which Rita kept well hidden. Now, looking back as an adult, I realize it was unintentional emotional abuse. Marie was having the time of her life, and Rita was left to fend for herself under the watchful eye of her Grandmother. Hence Rita used her humor and salty wit to keep people at bay. I lived in a warm home full of love, but preferred to walk four houses down the street, past Leo's house, to Rita's and spend the night. I loved her dearly. Her mother Marie did an about face after the car accident and was a wonderful devoted mother-and she was Rita's mentor. We all watched in awe as she donated the rest of her life to her daughter.

Lisa Simpson Perkins
Through the eyes of a child I listen to Lisa describe her Aunt Rita:

Lisa said she was only ten years old when Rita suffered greatly in her car accident. Lisa fondly remembers with great admiration her Aunt Rita, who would drive to Orinda for the holidays, or anytime, showing up in her Cougar or sports car, always bearing wrapped gifts for both her and her brother, Loren. Lisa remembers her slender aunt wearing Capris and a cotton blouse, her legs crossed, sitting at the end of the couch with a cigarette between her fingers and blowing smoke rings. Very sophisticated. Her Aunt Rita laughed easily and she remembers her witty comebacks. Her impression of Rita was that of a movie star who was a mystery. I warned Lisa: when you read her story you may learn more about your aunt than a niece needs to know. I laughed about some of the stories she'll read, and she said, "I can tell you two were friends; you sound like her, you speak like her." Lisa was a young impressionable niece who admired and watched her Aunt from a young girl's vantage point. Lisa still speaks very sweetly and highly of her sultry and sexy Aunt Rita.

NOTE: *Lisa graduated from college with a degree in Therapeutic Recreation, specializing in head injuries, RTR. Her interest and education sprouted from her love for her Aunt Rita.*

*Friends mentioned in this book
fondly remembered:*

Norman Moore and Beverly Perkins

www.ingramcontent.com/pod-product-compliance
Lightning Source LLC
Chambersburg PA
CBHW050555170426
43201CB00011B/1697